On Trees

Stella Longland

a Cave of Clay book

Copyright © Stella Longland 2018

Cover design by Stella Longland ©

second edition 2018
with text revisions

All rights reserved. No part of this publication may be reproduced, stored in a retrieval system, or transmitted in any form or by any means without prior written permission of the copyright owner. Nor can it be circulated in any form of binding or cover other than that in which it is published and without similar condition including this condition being imposed on a subsequent purchaser.

(first edition 2012 copyright © Stella Longland 2012)

British Library Cataloguing in Publication Data
A catalogue record for this book is available from the British Library

ISBN 978-1-9999024-2-1

The images of the birds were sourced from www.shutterstock.com
The Treecreeper is reproduced courtesy of FotoVeto
The Tawny Owl is reproduced courtesy of Grant Glendinning
The Great Spotted Woodpecker is reproduced courtesy of David Dohnal
The photographs of the Trees are by Stella Longland

On Trees

- oh -- ii -

- becoming teachable
I travel through time seeking awareness -

dedicated
to the spirit of
Elizabeth Longland
in thanks for her courage
and for the gift she gave to me

This story was written from the texts of audio tapes
recorded in a state of consciousness somewhere between
the worlds beyond and the world of everyday

Contents:

Year One

    Out of the Blue

Year Two

    The Protection of Trees

Year Three

    My Dance is a Tree

Year Four

    The Ascending Spiral

Year Five

    The Tree is Never Separated

Year Six

    From the Vast Form of the Earth

a path through the forest

Consult the final 5 pages to find
    About Teachers
    About a Paradox
    About Time and the Timeless
    Other Books by the Author
    Index of Contents and Images

Year One

When this story began, it was two years since my sister-in-law, Liz, the wife of my youngest brother, had been diagnosed with breast cancer. The doctors' prognosis was three months of life.

Amid flurries of snow, we buried her on a bitterly cold day in January. Defeating all expectations, she had lived for eighteen months; during that time, she had several visits from a group of spiritual healers and I noticed how much those sessions helped her. So it was that, after she died, I joined a spiritual healing group close to where I lived in north Yorkshire.

Out of the Blue

It was during a seminar, run by the leader of the healing group, on channelling spiritual guidance that an experience came to me, literally, out of the blue. We were working in pairs; one of us would enter an altered state while the other would ask questions to help us to vocalise what was happening and in this way capture any experiences that we had while in trance.

"Where are you?" said my partner, a gentle woman slightly younger than me. I was in the borderland; to my left was the forest, to my right, the grass plain. I answered her: "Watching animals running. They are beautiful." "Are you alone?" "No, I am never alone." "Who is with you? Is it your guide?" "It's my friend." For a while nothing was said. Then, she enquired: "Are you still there?" "No" I replied. I was silent as I wondered how to describe the place where I was finding myself; silent until I felt able to say: "I am somewhere yellow."

Something in the room distracts me: "Oh, I have come back. I will try to go down again. Will you help me?" "Relax, relax, go back now, go back. .... Where are you now?" "On a path." "What sort of path?" "A path through the forest." After being silent for a while my partner asks: "Do you like trees?" With slight amazement at this odd question, I reply emphatically: "I LOVE trees!" As soon as I speak these words all the trees vanish and there is only blackness. Horror struck, I cry out loudly: "Oh no, no!"

I hear the seminar leader come over and say: "Come on now, you must get through this." But I am already through. I have been 'kicked', that is the only way I can describe what happened, into extremely strong and all-embracing blue light, vivid, vivid blue light, brighter than the bluest sky; and in all directions, in front and behind, left and right, above and below, there is only blue light. I can feel my rapid eye movements, I am looking all around, and I am seeing only crystal-clear blue light; seeing with my eyes as if my eyes are open but I know that they are shut.

Yes, and I take time to check it out, slowly, consciously, behind those closed eyelids, moving my eyes in their sockets and, where there would usually be nothing to see, palpably seeing transparent blue light. I tell him: "Blue light, blue light!" "Is the blue light a problem?" he asks. "No," I reply: "the blue light is the breakthrough."

I sat up, completely present in the room. My partner asked: "Are you alright?" "Yes." I replied and the seminar leader left us on our own again. "I will try to go back." I lay down and drifted. "Where are you now?" I was in a circular place and trees were all around me. I knew they were trees but they were translucent, translucent crystal spires, silvery in the light, and very, very tall. Inside the circle that they made everything was yellow, rich, rich yellow going towards orange.

"Are there other people there?" "Yes, they are all here but not separate." .... "Are you afraid?" "I am indestructible." ...... "Can they speak to you?" "We do not speak here." .... "What is it like?" "It is like being part of an egg yolk." That was the colour, the vibrant yellow of a fresh egg yolk, and the surrounding trees were like the translucent egg white, which is the protection for the yolk. I knew no words to describe what it was like being there and, marvelling, I expressed my feelings in this way: "Why would anyone leave this place? Why would anyone leave this place?" But I knew that I had left and I said to my partner: "I will come back now. I will come back into the room."

A few months later, at the beginning of winter, I attended another weekend seminar. This time, a friend and colleague of the healing group leader, a person who explored the mysteries of sound, came to teach certain parts of the work. As I listened to him, singing overtones, on the first evening, I heard a switch click in my head and it seemed that the lights came on. The experiences I had over the next two days were so profound that, a week after the seminar, I wrote to him asking if he would be my Teacher. He replied with a yes, the indications were right and he accepted me.

He lived at the Findhorn Foundation and in order to attend the seminars he led there I would first need to participate in an experience week. This week would introduce me to the principles and practices of the community, so that when I attended courses I would already be familiar with the way of life and could focus more completely on the work to be done. I booked a place and the next month, in the first week of the new year there I was.

Year Two

On the first morning, I went to the nine o'clock meditation in the main sanctuary in the Park. The subject was 'Healing' and the person leading the meditation suggested that we speak out the names of the people for whom we were seeking help. After a struggle with embarrassment, I managed to whisper: "Wendy," the name of the wife of my doctor and a customer of my business who is very ill with breast cancer. About twenty seconds later, another woman's voice rang out clearly: "Wendy."

I felt ashamed that I could only whisper. I had the commitment but, well, I did not have the courage. I realized I had a long way to go in my healing quest. I tried to excuse myself by thinking that the whole world needed healing, I mean, every person in the world, as well as earth healing, and I felt the task was too big. It soon became clear to me that if I could not speak out for Wendy there was no point in my thinking on any bigger scale. The message was; just do what you are able to do, don't think you can do it all. It is not the first time I have had that insight, so I must try harder to put it into action. But what can I do?

When the meditation was over, I swiftly left the room to wipe my eyes. Thinking I was rushing to the next session, a young woman, who could hardly speak English, followed me out and we went together to the next activity, a class on sacred dancing.

The woman who was teaching us the dances was my mother reincarnated. My mother loved to dance, but she was short and plump, serious impediments to having a professional dancing career. As a child, I was a promising dancer and my mother had hopes for me but, when I was ten, I broke my elbow so badly that my arm could never be straight. In consequence, dancing lessons were given up as having little point; it might have been better for me if I had been encouraged to continue dancing for the joy of it. All this history went through my mind as we began the session. The dancing was gentle, lyrical and nurturing; slowly any pain eased away. This nearly brought me to tears again, but I opted for gratitude to the spirit of the Foundation instead.

Later that day, our mentors took us by bus to Cluny College, another part of the Foundation a few miles away. The participants in the introductory week, putting into practice the tenet 'work is love in action', would spend three half-days working as community members. We went to the sanctuary there to pick our angel for the week and to choose our workplaces through meditation.

During the meditation that preceded choosing the angel card I connected to a higher level, I could see a higher plain but I was not on it. Two guides seemed to reach down towards me in colours. The feminine one, on the right, came with black and purple, and the masculine one, on the left, came in golden yellow and brown. They descended and, as they reached out for me, the three of us made a Y-shape. Touching me, they twisted round each other into a multi-coloured spiral of yellow, black, purple, and brown.

After meditating, we picked our cards. I got 'Expectancy'. I was a bit surprised; I felt that I might have come with expectations that were too high, and people have often told me that I expect too much, but maybe, now, that would be ok. For the rest of the week I worked to unravel the emotional legacy living in me, a legacy passed down from my female ancestors, and I sought to identify, to observe, and to understand its effects on me. This work had to be done because, in a society on fast forward, some of that legacy was less of an ancestral survival strategy and more of a curse.

Two dreams illustrate what I needed to unpick. The setting for both was on the farm where I was born, close to the barns where the bales were stored after the harvest.

In the first, which came before I began experience week, I was with a woman larger and bossier than me, we were running an enterprise together, a smallholding. Someone was visiting and the three of us were chatting when the overbearing woman declared with great satisfaction: "We got rid of our fox!" Yes, we had got rid of 'our' fox and I was pleased too. "How did you manage that?" the visitor asked. "Oh," she said: "he used to dance in that spare bit of ground by the dutch barns. He was so happy dancing, he wasn't taking notice and someone managed to shoot him from the other side of the river." My feeling of achievement vanished and my sense of shared mood collapsed; the fox had been shot from land owned by someone else but, worse, worst of all, he had been shot when he was dancing. A shocking, dreadful, sacrilegious crime had been committed and I was a party to it. I came back fast and woke up weeping.

The second dream came a couple of weeks later, after I left the Foundation, in about two pages time!

On the last day of the week, when we finished our morning's work, we had a tuning-out session where we picked blessings cards. The card I picked was 'Optimism'. I am optimistic: smiling happily I remembered that the angel card was 'Expectancy': "Expectancy and Optimism, these are qualities I have and that people can find annoying in me, but I feel, I have always felt, that they are good qualities to have." A rush of emotion hit me, I bent my head down to contain its effect because I was overwhelmed by having the qualities I cherish endorsed in this way; no longer did they seem like a child's act of defiance.

We finished tuning-out, it was late and I rushed to the sanctuary to join the meditation at noon. The subject of the meditation was 'Love'. I looked for Love, the selfless love I might have given and received in my life. Only two instances came to my mind: one was for my baby, that was the love I gave, and the other was the love that I received when, only recently, I felt the presence of a spirit guide. Those two loves were comparable, but nothing else came near to unconditional love.

The death of my sister-in-law had been the last in a series of events, including the death of my mother two years earlier, which had caused my world-view to fall apart. This falling apart was accompanied by excruciatingly painful physical experiences whose origins were unknown. Along with them came unexpected changes. I had thrived on stress since my mid-teens, it was my motivation to get things done, but suddenly it was not possible for me to live like that any longer and I only understood that I needed to change fast. In the sanctuary, meditating on unconditional love, I saw that, although I had longed for love, I had not been loveable. I realized that until my world-view disintegrated I was not open to the world of love and this final realization was truly devastating.

It is very challenging to weep uncontrollably during a silent meditation in a room full of people. Tears were cascading out of my eyes and pouring down my nose and I could only breathe with my mouth open. Earlier in the day, someone at work had painted our faces with beetroot juice and I realized that by now I must look like something out of a horror movie. The thought of my appearance made me laugh: life was terrible but wonderful at the same time. I felt justified, devastated, and grateful all at the same time. After the meditation, I went to wash the beetroot off my face. Someone in the cloakroom saw what a state I was in, but, and this is the great thing about the Findhorn Foundation, it was no big deal.

I went for a walk to clear my mind. Behind Cluny College, which was originally a hotel, there is a hillock and the way to the top is along a spiral path.

the spiral mound

I walked up the spiral, and on the top, I found a silver birch tree with two close-growing trunks. It was not a big tree, the trunks were only about the diameter of my thighs, and I jammed myself in between them. The sun was shining onto the tree; the light was intense. There was a terrific wind blowing, terrific, and it really was impossibly warm for January. The two parts of the tree were moving in the wind, nudging and supporting me. Suddenly I sang to them. When I sang to the first trunk, the wind came through in a great roar. It was brilliant, just like the light. When I sang to the second trunk something numinous happened because of the wind blowing and the song singing and the love that was generated there. So I made an invocation to spirit: "I will listen. I will listen to the spirit world. I will quieten my ego. I will listen. For goodness' sake send me some messages so I can find the path." Then I disentangled myself and walked down. That is what happened on the spiral mound and I came down feeling very different.

In the second dream, I was walking up the lane along the side of the green wood with the dutch barns and farm fields to my left. I looked up and some distance ahead, where the wood came to an end and the pasture began, a very large male lion, with a truly outstanding shaggy mane, was standing at the corner of the wood. Not looking towards me, head erect he was scenting the air. I stared; a truly magnificent creature, much, much larger than me, about four times the size of any lion I had ever seen. What was he doing there? How had he got there? Where had he come from? And what should I do?

I had two choices, sidestep into the wood and try to disappear, or stay exactly where I was. Doing neither, I stepped to the right and stood with my back against the trees. The maned lion was still in sight. I thought: "I'm on the path now, so perhaps he won't hurt me." This was a challenge: would I be proved correct? Trying to become less noticeable, I crouched down with my back to the wood and, afraid to turn my head, stared straight forward. Soon I saw, out of the corner of my eye, that the lion was walking towards me. I was absolutely petrified; he certainly might eat me. I was determined to stay right there and I just shut my eyes tight, hoping, if I didn't make a challenge with eye contact, that he might ignore me.

I hardly breathed as the long seconds passed. Any moment I expected to feel the jaws around my head crushing the life out of me. I could not hear any movement yet I knew he was right in front of me, coming so close I could smell him, an overwhelming, pungent, nostril-tingling smell, once smelt as a child in the lion house at London Zoo and so always to be viscerally remembered. I stayed there frozen for what seemed like ages. When I eventually plucked up courage to open my eyes, the lion had gone. I immediately woke up.

How often has my sense of smell been active in a dream? I can't think of another circumstance. That lion was real, more real than the familiar background I had grown up in, but I didn't run away and I didn't even hide! I didn't get killed either. I had faced up to something. I had achieved something, which perhaps, in time, would be understood.

Back at home, a few months later in early spring, the weather was so beautiful, calm, blue; so beautiful, that after work I felt compelled to go for a walk. I really wanted to go to the wood just a few fields away from my house to see if the bluebells, which grew there in abundance, were in bloom, and to sit there with a particular silver birch tree, so, I walked there. I easily found the tree. Although a young slim tree the trunk is very tall, putting my arms around it I leaned backwards and looked up at the branches all clustered in the canopy of the wood. The leaf buds were beginning to burst and the tops of the trees meeting there made intricate and colourful patterns against the blue, so much closer to the sky than me.

I lay down there to meditate, but I could hardly bear to close my eyes because the place was so beautiful. I drifted. I thought about the beauty of nature, the power rising up the trees, the birds singing, yes, it was glorious. I felt I was letting my guides hear the sounds of this world through my ears. I felt they were listening for things they recognised.

It came to me that trees are channels for the Earth's energy, and help the planet to live. Then I thought that maybe people could be channels of energy in a similar way, there followed the interesting idea that individually we have the same importance as a single tree.

birch trees in a spring sky

The next month my Teacher came again, to the town near where I lived, to give another seminar with the leader of the healing group. We took a drum journey to meet our power animal and I chose to go to a marvellous tree that I know.

I first found it in the winter on a still frosty day of brilliant sunshine. I didn't know what sort of tree it was, but it was a beautiful shape. The trunk was straight and broad to a height of eight feet; above that the branches, growing out from the central trunk at shallow angles, spread wider and wider forming a large circle in the high canopy of the wood and creating a similar clear circular space on the ground below. In the uppermost branches, there was a squirrels' nest. I sat and watched five grey squirrels romping through the branches and racing up and down the trunk, bounding into the adjacent trees in a rush of january joy.

the tree in winter

Next time I visited, the tree was in full flower. The lower branches were bare; the upper branches that could reach the light were a mass of pink blossom, a glorious, glorious sight. The air was full of the sound of bees and other insects indulging in a pollen frenzy. I could tell, from the flowers and the emerging leaves, what type of tree it was, an Apple tree, a forty-foot high Apple tree, but I could hardly believe an Apple tree could grow that big; it must be ancient.

So, that is where I went. I stood there for a long time watching the squirrels. Then I noticed the Coyote to my left: the Coyote, my guardian, my travelling helper. How? Why? Well, that is another story. He looked at the squirrels leaping around and he said: "This is fun! Let's hunt one. How are we going to get up there?"

At that very moment, the ground began to shake and the Coyote ran to a hole, shouting: "Hurry up! Hurry up! The ground is moving." I thought: "It's not much good going into a hole in the ground if the ground is moving." But the hole wasn't in the ground, it was in the sky and it wasn't so much a hole as a square box in the sky. It was like an old safe, the sort that has really thick metal walls, hanging in the sky. The door was missing: bank robbery came to mind. We scrambled up and crouched in this safe in the sky, peering over the edge, watching the ground ripple and buckle.

The Coyote said: "There's going to be a change." And I saw that the trees were the cause of the rippling of the ground. They were going to become Walking Beings and the earth was being shaken like a blanket by the trees pulling up their roots. For as far as I could see, right to the horizon, the green and brown landscape was rolling and heaving because the trees were lifting their legs out of the ground and walking off. The world was full of trees stumping away, stumping off to do their own thing.

He said: "There's going to be a change. Now people are going to be trees. I'll be the ground." And he laid himself down as the yellow ground. I became a tree; my roots went into him and my branches went up. He said: "You can drop seeds on me and I'll grow them for you." I dropped some. They were like sycamore seeds, twirling down, striking the ground and driving themselves into the coyote-soil. I stretched my branches up to the blue sky. I reached towards it with joy. I worshipped the sky. I felt great and still, calm and peaceful. I thought: "Now the squirrels can come and live in me and we shan't have to kill them." On the way home from the seminar at the end of that day I visited the Apple tree. I asked the tree to help me. I came home, and I am going to try to sleep and get my equilibrium back so that tomorrow I can function in the daily world, if that is possible.

Another month went by before I printed a story I had written to send to my Teacher. I decided to go for a walk before writing a note to go with it. I went and lay in the bluebell wood for an hour or more. Again, the wood in late spring was so beautiful I found it hard to close my eyes and go to another world, this one seemed good enough.

I came out of the wood and walked towards a mature Ash tree, planted in the open field as shelter for farm animals, a tawny owl flew out of it. That was strange because it was not yet twilight. As I came closer to the tree I saw a very small rabbit, about four weeks old, sat in the grass. Had the owl been hunting the rabbit? I walked closer, but the rabbit did not run until I was about three feet away, then it popped down a nearby burrow. I looked up at the tree. There, about seven feet off the ground, sat on a branch, was a young owl not yet fully fledged. I saw that it was not able to fly so the nest must be in that tree. I looked at it and it stared straight back at me. I was so stunned to have such a close view that I sat down to watch it, not that it did much.

There was a ditch between me and the tree, the owlet, and the rabbit, and there were some rabbit holes in the bank. I saw a movement inside one hole; the opening was large as the edges of the hole had collapsed, the sun was low and shining in, but it was not the rabbit that I saw inside, it was a weasel. The weasel was darting backwards and forwards, hunting in the tunnels. No wonder the little rabbit had been reluctant to go below ground, in fact, it had come back out. So, there was the owl above, the rabbit in the middle, and the weasel below. Three power animals within a few feet of each other, not bad for a walk in the english countryside.

the tree of the animals

It was a Sunday, I had a full day to spend as I pleased, and so I drove the few miles to the local Fell and went for a wonderful walk on that vast area of moorland in limestone country. At first sight the moor may look like a wasteland, but it is full of amazing geological formations and cut by deep, tree-filled gullies. At one particular place a river, having run underground for much of its course in the upland parts of the Fell where only the rock-strewn river bed shows its occasional course, rises above ground in a sparkling torrent of waterfalls and dark pools.

This day I walked along the top of the ridge above the river valley to where the ditches and banks of an Iron Age hill-fort are still visible. An outraged sheep stared at me; it was comical, I was not expected there. I walked on to a gulley that a small beck, taking water to the river below, has carved out. Rarely would anyone visit there, except occasionally, perhaps, a farmer looking for lost sheep.

the tree over the water

An Ash tree stands there, the main trunk grows out over the water at right angles to the bank, and several secondary trunks grow from the same point in different directions so that the tree forms a shape not unlike a bowl.

The main limb of the trunk is flat and broad, you could lie on it, but I didn't because it was a very slippery day. Instead, I climbed down the steep bank beneath the tree and crossed to a flat area on the other side of the beck. The main limb grew out, over this patch of ground, and my head was underneath it. On the opposite bank, at my eye level, the roots of the tree, exposed by erosion, were visible. I was looking at them when I felt, with surprise, strong magnetic pulses. How they were generated I did not know, but I noticed that my upper body was circling on the spot.

Feeling this unknown energy, I asked the tree to help me, but the problem was that the minute I stood still ten million midges came to torment me. This is what I'm finding about this meditating out in nature. It is a joke. Things bite me, I itch, things drop unexpectedly off trees and land on me, sheep make the most appalling racket! I felt the power of the place, but I couldn't meditate there.

There was another tree a little farther up the beck. Maybe that was a bit more in the breeze. On reaching it, I discovered that it is a dual tree, a rowan and a sallow grown together so that, although the leafy branches still declare their separate origins, their trunks are indistinguishably one. But, even though the wind was stronger, the midges were still impossible.

Climbing out of the gulley, I went on up the ridge to a ruined house and sat under the huge sycamore tree, which once gave shade to a farmyard, growing there. It began to rain heavily. This deterred the midges and, snug and dry in waterproof jacket and trousers, I stayed there until the shower was over. Then I went down to the valley bottom where, on a sharp bend in the river, there is a wide-spreading oak tree.

I stopped there by a waterfall, looking at the sheer black rock face opposite, watching the water running down it. The rocks I was standing on were like glass, dangerous, if I had fallen and injured myself I would have lain a long time before anyone came by, and nobody knew where I was.

I perched there and sang the five creative sounds, -ah, -eh, -ii, -oh, -uu, as taught by Joseph Rael, writer of books on the mysteries of sound. I sang them, wobbly at first, then louder and louder, until they were very loud. At last, surrounded by the noise of the waterfall, I had found a place to sing. I sang: "-uu" and opened my eyes. In front of me the rocks were all moving in waves, whether that was caused by a lack of oxygen or something else, I do not know.

As I walked back to the car, taking the shorter route through a wood, the rain came on again. This time it was torrential; this time, running in streams down my waterproofs, it filled my walking boots. I didn't take shelter, I didn't mind; I had found a place, close to home, where I could develop my voice and where I would surely learn amazing things.

It was my Teacher, Alexander, who had introduced me to the five primal sounds. Joseph had visited the Foundation while travelling and teaching in Europe; he found Alexander there, spent the afternoon with him, asked for a tape recorder, made him a cassette, told him he was a chanter and left. Now I was becoming a chanter too. Close to the village that gives the river its name, I found that two great trees had recently fallen over the path.

two fallen trees

A yellow dog ran past me. I said hello to the man who accompanied it. We walked along together and chatted, he confided to me: "I am a Christian. You may not believe this, but I really needed a job, I prayed to God for a job and within a fortnight I got one." I nodded and said: "Oh, I can believe it."

This morning, as I lay in bed, I remembered that some powerful things happened on the walk yesterday, and last night it felt like things, which I could not understand, were going on in my energy field, so, I decided to walk the walk again, in meditation. I visited the Iron Age fort. Walking on, I arrived at the Ash tree and decided to stay there. The tree materialized as if it was real and I entered into deep contact with it. The pulsing magnetic energy, I had felt the day before, was very present. I experienced deep changes of body state and an awareness of my psyche questing outwards: unusual, interesting, wonderful. Thank you to that tree, to that tree and to the running water.

At the healing group, we once went on a guided meditation to the summer lands with similar imagery, for example, there was a waterfall, and that had worked to a degree for me. But yesterday, somehow, I must have picked up the force field of the living tree and it came back to me this morning like a reality. It is a quietly impressive event.

I shut my eyes, emptied my mind, and after a long time the image of a tree came and embraced me. It was the hollow Ash tree where I saw the three animals: rabbit, owl, and weasel. I entered the feeling of that tree and the sandy-coloured Coyote gave me some advice, saying quietly: "Channel healing. When other people channel voices, they believe in it and they do it. You've to do this when you're healing." He paused, and then said: "Do this when you are healing: imagine yourself to be the outside of a hollow tree and let all the golden light flow through. Let the golden light come through."

As a person running their own business, for many years I worked a seven-day week, but now I try with all my might to get out, get away, on my own into some remote place, every now and then. I am most often able to do this on a Sunday and this was another opportune Sunday; I went out walking early. I had decided to go and find the caves that are marked on the ordnance survey map of the Fell, a task I had the inspiration to do, but that I have failed to complete. I took a pair of secateurs because I also intended to visit the numinous Ash tree, which came to me in meditation with its energy field intact and without midges, and cut off the ivy that is growing up one of the secondary trunks. I went there first, walking over the tops until I reached the edge of the gulley.

Below me was the double tree, rowan and sallow growing as one. Everything was energetically charged and just right, so I sat down for a moment on a rock. Out of the corner of my eye, I saw something moving. I looked up to see a large buzzard fly low over the top of the gulley. Then it wheeled back and sailed behind the Ash tree, about thirty feet from me. It turned on its side, wings outstretched and showed me its belly, all the feathers dappled and barred. It sailed slowly past the tree, rose into the sky, folded back its wings, and dropped like a stone out of sight, stooping after some quarry, some poor unsuspecting rabbit. I have never seen a buzzard so close; I must be doing something right.

I stood up and went down to the dual tree to look in the limpid pool beside it. I put my hands in and touched my forehead with the water. I looked across the surface of the water and there, on the other side, slightly to my left, was the entrance to an underground world. The opening was quite dry inside and, looking really inviting, it ran away underneath the tree roots, but I was far too big to crawl in. Stretched across the entrance was the most beautifully spun spider's web. I put my hand in the water again and tapped my forehead three times with the cold water from the pool. Then I went to the Ash tree where I found the force field to be just as strong as it had been previously. Afraid that the ivy will eventually kill the tree I tried to cut it off, but I soon realized that I need to take a pruning saw.

I left the gulley and walked a long way up the river, spectacular scenery but no sign of caves. Eventually I turned back, stopping for a while to sing the five vowel sounds, sitting by the waterfall above the pool where I had sung them before. Singing the sound '-eh', my voice was wobbly and I found that I was out of line with my placement. My problem is accepting that I am not going to be able to see my Teacher very often, a seven-hour journey. I felt a wave of dissatisfaction. I knew I had to overcome it because it is not about getting what I want; it is about doing what I need to do.

Tonight is the regular Friday evening meeting of the healing group where we meditate and practice healing. Some people in the group also do channelling, and we all have an opportunity to ask the channelled guide questions. This morning I drove out to visit a customer and, while I was driving, I re-lived the part of the drum journey where I was watching the squirrels playing in the Apple tree. I particularly recalled the Coyote saying: "This is fun, let's hunt one!" This troubles me. I wonder whether it is an expression of a deep desire of mine, or whether it is only the Coyote who has that desire. So I was thinking: "Where does the killing urge come from?" when a grey squirrel shot out from a driveway straight under the front of the car. The front wheels missed it, but the back wheel on the driver's side killed it stone dead. I looked in the wing mirror, its body, thrown out from under the wheel, was rolling in the road like a rag. Something seemed to say to me: "Once you killed animals for food, now you just kill them."

The dynamic in the group that evening was likely to be complicated, the group leader was encouraging people to try channelling, and I knew I had to remain very calm. So, in the opening meditation, I went to a familiar place; the bungalow that the Coyote is renovating for me, but that is another story. Arriving there I carefully kissed the door posts and I felt very dizzy: I knew that I had entered an altered state. Looking down to keep my balance, I crossed over the threshold. I noticed that the 'Welcome' mat was placed so that I would read it as I left, a welcome, not on coming in but on going out! I spent some time thinking about how the message applied placed like that. I concluded that I don't need to be welcomed on entering my own house, but that it is different when I step into the world outside; that is where the strangers are. Walking further along the hallway I went to the newel post, which stands alone because the staircase is not yet built, but one day, I have been assured, there will be an upper floor. In going there, my thought was: "The newel post will be the place where there will be the most power to help me stay calm." And, yes, as I approached, it became a large hollow tree and I went in, in to a vast land. It was a delightful land, and I didn't want to come out of that space, but I did, when the group leader called us.

As we paired up to practice healing, I noticed that an odd number of people were present and I volunteered to sit out. While I sat there I meditated and found, not for the first time, that I was participating in the healing. I could sense a beam of light leaving me that focused on a person and added something to help the healer. The beam is not generated by my effort; it comes from an unknown external source. I can tell that because I feel entranced, stuck with glue to the task in hand, and, to keep my attention, interesting images, colours, and vague, difficult-to-grasp impressions, run through my head while it is happening.

Next, a member fairly new to the group channelled her guide. I sensed danger there, there was something too present about the channeller, and interpretations of other people's spiritual business were too readily given. To a question, the answer was: "You only have one previous human incarnation and your house is in a bad spot." I felt that was not at all helpful. This particular channeller has no qualms about dominating others, but, thankfully, I notice, she treats me with caution.

Even so, when her channelling finished I felt knocked out psychically, and, addressing the invisible Beings, I said: "I think I need help." The Medicine Man, whose colours are black and white, came and showed me his shield, which had knotted black leather straps hanging from it, I focused on it and he brought it right up to my face so that it blocked everything else out. Rather interesting, a psychic shield that stopped me being drawn into a challenging area, it meant that I was able to ask penetrating questions and to listen and to judge. I must say I never felt this need of protection before. Although the main channelled guide for the group sometimes bores the pants off me, I missed him at this session very much, and I understood and appreciated what a controlled force for good he is. And, on this evening, I also understood and appreciated the integrity of the person who channels him.

The evening always ends with a cup of tea and cake, but one of the group members, someone who was already an experienced channel, needed to leave early. As soon as she had left, something happened that I could not understand. The group leader asked in a very gleeful voice: "Who thinks she is going to leave the group then?" I was shocked. What sort of group activity was this, discussing someone's future like that? Everyone, except me, said that she would leave. I only said that I would like her to stay. It was as if the leader had found a promising substitute and was pushing her out. I don't quite understand the deeper motivations and causes of this, but I can see that it is not all positive.

Now it is Saturday morning, I had a good night's sleep and yet I felt very tired when I woke up and the meditation this morning was challenging. The guide I now call 'Grandfather', whose colours are golden yellow and brown, spoke to me, saying: "You have to sort out what happened last night. Detach yourself and re-establish your equilibrium." Yes, the meeting of the healing group last night was not easy, so I paused and focused my attention. I decided I would go and look within myself, and I went down into a deep pit where I fought my way through the dynamics of the group, the personality disputes, the power struggles, the turmoil, and confusion. I struggled with it all for some time but, when I opened my eyes to come out of that place, I still didn't feel good, I still didn't feel settled, and I went back to try again.

The Grandfather and his companion, the Medicine Man, lifted me up into the branches of a tree, the tree swayed gently in the wind and I was gently swayed. Relaxing there, I thought of the squirrel, of the inevitability of death: an inescapable part of the world of everyday. When I was in the pit I couldn't accept that, it gave me the horrors, but up in the tree it was less significant and when I left the tree I felt better. I am calm now and back to my strength. This is one of the tests, I see. It is all very well telling myself I am connected to other worlds and that I can cope with daily life, but get out there and mingle. Find out what it's like, hell. Hell. Enter other people's hells. Enter their hells and come out intact. That's hard. Watch and watch out. Watch out how they stir up your own hells.

On my way to the Wednesday evening healing session that our group offered each week in a local hall, I stopped the car and went into the wood where the Apple tree grows. I intended to find a particular tree whose branches make a good seat and sit there for a while. I felt on edge. It is eight weeks since the seminar and since I heard from my Teacher, and that is causing me to be a bit impatient. Well, could I find that tree? I could not find it. Last time I sat there, I cried and cried, and worked through a problem that was also related to not being able to work more closely with him. Maybe the tree had had enough of my crying and hid itself.

At one point in my search, I passed a spot that was powerful, so I lay down with my forehead to the ground and the Coyote tried to explain to me what is going on. He hinted that I should not gnaw this bone so intensely, and gave me various alternative ways of approaching the situation. He made it quite clear that a wide space has to be maintained between us human Beings or else the work will not go right. I half understood, half accepted that I should not get wound up, but the side of me that is impatient and discontent was on the up.

I went on to the mid-week healing. There were about ten people attending. In preparation for the healing sessions, I meditated on Peace. Peace was the energy that I was lacking. Words came to me from the depths; 'Patience', 'Acceptance', 'Calmness', and I noticed that their first letters were close in sound to the word 'PAX', the latin word for peace, so, from my thinking mind, in order to make the sound 'pacs', I added one word that started with S. However, this word beginning with S is the one word I cannot recall, maybe it was 'Serenity' or 'Silence'; I can't be sure. If a thing comes to me from the deep place and I lose it, I can return there and find it, but if it comes from the surface of my mind it has no place in the timeless and there is nowhere to look for it. If I create it on the surface and wish to be able to find it again, then I have to place it into timelessness, otherwise it will be ephemeral. This placement is a conscious act.

Are we like this? If we don't connect consciously to deep

levels, are we ephemeral? Searching for something less fleeting, and maybe because I had been in the wood, I visualized myself as a tree, but there was a pain in the centre of my chest which distracted me. There was a knot there. I told this knot to go away: "Knot of anxiety, knot of impatience, go away." Then I realized that trees are full of knots and they just grow around them; knots are part of the tree. I continued the visualization during the healing sessions and that was very good as my hands were like branches stirred by the wind and my body pushed energy with that springy resistance that you feel in the trees.

At the end of the evening, the group leader asked me if I would be in charge of the healing on the Wednesday of the next week. He said I was the best person for holding the spiritual energy when he is away. I felt I didn't really want to do it but, on reflection, I felt happy that he had that confidence in me and I said I would. He was not able to be at the coming Friday meeting either, but I didn't want to go to that. Without him, they usually talk about reading tea leaves and other types of prediction and I am not interested in that. I decided to go for a walk on the Fell instead.

I knew I was in a troubled state, the most dissatisfied psychological state I've been in for a long time, and I wanted to take the time to work through my emotional distress. Taking the pruning saw with me to cut the ivy, I walked to the Ash tree in the gulley, but, when I got there, I did not use it. I wrestled instead with the problem of messing with a sacred place, of trying to control nature. I lay on the horizontal trunk and thought about the movement of spirit power in the world and of my vision where the trees went into blackness. Was the correct interpretation that something catastrophic would happen to them caused by us? The breeze was strong, causing the branches to move and the leaves to rattle, then suddenly the wind would drop and there would be complete quiet, just like I experience sometimes when I'm meditating and all my body noises cease. It was very restful and peaceful, but I wasn't at peace.

I announced my troubles, trying to grasp the reasons why I am so unhappy; then I jumped up and walked north to where the ground gradually climbs and the river drops underground. As I strode along, the Coyote suddenly spoke to me, saying in a casual tone: "A name of mine is Wenif; it contains some teaching about the relationship between predestination and free will." After a significant pause for me to catch up, he continued: " 'When' is a definite moment in time and space, 'if' is a psychological possibility, and when the two coincide, things happen as they should." I liked the name and the concept made me laugh; 'when' is a definite: that's predestination, 'if' is a possibility and that is free will. And that's it: the paradox. He said: "When you reach a paradox, that's the place to stop." And I sat down for a while. A beautiful, healthy, bushy grey squirrel appeared on the opposite bank and searched for food, unthreatened by, and unafraid of, me. Soon it bounded out of sight.

Standing up, I walked down into the dry river bed and chose a big boulder to sit on. The images in my mind were strongly affected by the place, becoming very slow and immutable. I took a bottle of water and poured libations to the four points of the compass. I apologised for my faults and asked for assistance to transform them into something helpful. To conclude the ceremony, I took four mouthfuls of water. I climbed out of the gulley and fought my way through heather, bracken and all other obstacles until I reached the road. The minute my foot touched the tarmac, it began to pour down with rain. I am having a tormented time. I am feeling angry and disappointed with myself. I will see what tomorrow brings. Tomorrow brought a bad hormonal headache, so maybe that is where the turmoil originated.

    The following Wednesday I ran the healing. A mother and son were there. I channelled healing to the mother. She seemed very calm, but she had told me that she had a lump in her left upper chest which the doctors were about to investigate, and as I encountered it I got a bad feeling, it seemed to have its own energy field. I hope the healing helped her. On the way home, I sat in the wood in front of the Apple tree. It was a very still night and just warm enough; the stillness, the power of the motionless trees, the birds moving quietly around. I gave thanks, kissed the earth and came back home.

    Despite hideous weather, I went for a walk on Sunday. It had rained all day but I needed exercise and air; I was not feeling well. I decided to try to find the 'missing' tree seat in the Apple tree wood. I found the tree, it was further away than I had remembered, and I sat down. There were lots of flies, lots of midges and lots of large raindrops falling occasionally, suddenly. I sat for a while. The flies walked on me and the midges pricked my skin. It was hideous. I swatted them all. Suddenly the Coyote whispered to me: "If you really loved me, you would lie down here and meditate." I remonstrated: "Here? It's impossible." "Ah, but if you really loved me you would overcome all these things." Ridiculous: "I am just joking with myself, making life hard for myself, giving myself guilt." Then I thought: "But I do want to prove to myself, if not to the Coyote, that I am prepared to put myself out." So I lay down flat on my back, put my hat over my eyes, and determined to stick with it. It soon got very pleasant. The flies disappeared, the midges couldn't get through my socks, which I had pulled up, and when the big drops fell they always did so with immaculate timing, coinciding with some shift in the meditation.

I wanted to see the Coyote badly, but which manifestation? He has many: sandy-yellow, black, or nebulous; running on all fours, or standing on hind legs and walking like a man, to name but a few. So I said: "I want to see you, Coyote, but you choose, come as anything you like." There was a long pause. Then he said: "I don't choose to come as any thing. I choose to come as no thing. Where in your world can you find nothing?" Another long pause ensued while I thought and thought: "Where in this world is nothing? This world only exists in things." Suddenly I had an inspiration: "No thing exists in me." It was the right answer. "Then I will come into you." And he came in to my non-existence, and I saw him within, very, very nice, very, very deep contact and very much fun too. Thank you, Coyote!

I did not go to the following Friday meeting; the group leader was still away and card readings were going to be done. I drove up the Fell as far as the road goes and from there I walked out onto the moor at about six o'clock. Alone in the wilderness, I had intended to do the usual Friday evening meditation practices, but I couldn't concentrate. I thought about the Earth, but I didn't go through the Earth healing meditation that had come through one of the group in a channelling session. Instead, I sat there, and tuned in and tuned in to the surroundings.

The weather was divine, blue sky and still air combining to create a great sense of peace. As the sun began to drop, I climbed up the hill to stay in its light. I didn't think where I was going, I followed a whim and I reached a place where another extraordinary Ash tree grows out of the heart of a rock. Growing from a vertical fissure, the trunk is wide and fat, pitted and short, about four feet wide at the top and only four feet high before it splits into a myriad of branches, the shape probably the result of constant cropping by sheep. The rock in which it is embedded is full of fissures and deep cracks and the tree is like the rock. The trunk faces directly towards the dropping summer sun.

the tree from rock

I put my head to the trunk to feel the essence of this tree: steadfast, benevolent, and enduring. At my feet, sheltered by the outreaching branches, there was an inviting grassy patch. I lay down there, on my back to start with, but the flies and the intense light made me decide to roll over and lie on my front. Immediately a deep feeling gripped me, and what a fight ensued!

"Relax into the ground," came the instruction from invisible guides. But I couldn't let go. It was a strong physical, weighty, sexual feeling, lying in the bright sunlight on the mossy ground beneath the great fat tree, and I just couldn't let go, couldn't allow this feeling to come into full expression, and because I wouldn't allow this feeling to express itself, I couldn't sink into the ground. The Coyote was pushing me, trying to help me. The Medicine Man came; they were both trying to push me in. Then the Grandfather arrived and suddenly I was in.

Once in, it was so clear that the ground loved and welcomed me that I relaxed completely. I haven't felt that sense of security and safety since I was a tiny child and, as the earth enveloped me, this memory that was lost to me returned in feeling. Held by the ground, I lay there until the sun went down behind the trees on the opposite side of the dry river gorge.

I got up and inspected the heart-shaped tree, I marvelled how it grew out of the rock; all earth is made of rock: it is the Tree of Earth. Then it came to me that the Ash tree in the gulley grows out over the water; it is the Tree of Water. The Ash tree where I saw the owl, the rabbit, and the weasel, is the Tree of Fire; the hollow trunk is scorched inside, a lightning-struck tree. The Tree of the Air may be still to come, or maybe I have already found it and have not realized. Now, months later, as I type up the tape, it is clear to me that the Tree of Air is the Apple tree.

I walked back to the car, but I didn't want to leave just yet. The luminous light of the setting sun was shining down the next valley; a track ran from where the car was parked towards this light. I walked along slowly, looking into the light. Suddenly I saw an animal bounding up the dark side of the Fell. It was a fox. It ran lightly and swiftly up the fell-side. As it ran, the birds flew up panicking and the young sheep scattered. Briefly disappearing from view, it re-appeared on the very top, silhouetted, black against the golden light, and ran along the ridge. I nearly died of joy. This was a very wonderful walk. Instead of sending the Earth healing, I had received earth healing in abundance.

The Protection of Trees

A muddled meditation this morning, I seemed to arrive at a tree but I didn't travel any further. I felt some physical changes of state. I drifted. Tried to get through some places; couldn't get through. I just didn't have it in me somehow. I think I was knocked out by yesterday evening on the Fell, time for some time off.

Somewhere during this meditation I heard the unmistakable sound of a bird hitting the window, it brought me to everyday consciousness. Later I went out to look along the front of the house and I found a small dead bird. I looked it up in a book of birds.

treecreeper

The distinctly curved beak identified it as a treecreeper, a bird that lives on and depends on trees, a bird that shelters in cracks in the bark of trees in the cold of winter in order to survive. Why would this tree hugging bird fly across the main road at a height of thirty feet to die against my window? I felt sad, another animal sacrifice.

I took the wings and tail and, attaching them to a piece of bark, I made an 'icon'. I don't know what the correct word would be: a totem, a meditation symbol, a sacred object, a material acknowledgement, a learning creation, the list could go on. I buried the rest, thanking the bird for its message, which strengthened my relationship with trees.

The next day, Sunday, I went for a walk up the lower reaches of the river, walking along the riverside path to the first waterfalls, intending afterwards to visit the Ash tree that grows out over the water. I stayed at the falls for a while and I went to the rock face to do some singing. Two young trees had fallen, perhaps in heavy rain. One, a birch, its top branches lying in the river, the leaves wilted, seemed to be dead. The other, a rowan, although it too was now lying head down the banking, still had green healthy leaves, and this reminded me again that rowan can survive the most extreme catastrophes and live with hardly any root in the ground.

The sight of these two, newly fallen, trees and the memory of the two trees that had fallen onto the path the previous month led me to ask myself: "What is death in relation to a tree?" Yes, when they stop living they stop growing, but that doesn't mean that they stop being. I thought of all the things a dead tree can become and all the ways they help us to survive. At the rock face I sang. I can't say it was brilliant. But feeling afterwards more at ease with myself and my place in the natural world, I spent some long time examining the oak tree that grows on the bend in the river and watching the motion of the water sliding over the edge of the waterfall and falling into the turbulence of the pool below.

the spreading oak tree

Then, leaving the river, I made my way to the Ash tree that grows in the gulley out over the waters of the beck. My inclination might be not to put what happened there on the tape, but I cannot allow my everyday self to act as censor, and so, in the interest of the full picture, I am going to record it.

As I approached, a bird left the top of the tree, flying fast without any sound. A bird with no neck, a blunt head, a fattish body, brown, with fairly long, broad wings; it went so quickly, I couldn't identify it. Then a second one left the tree; three wing beats, a glide, three more, then, passing over the far edge of the gulley, out of sight. I think, from the short necks that they must have been owls.

I felt the protecting presence of the tree embrace and surround me. The weather was warm and dry and I lay on my belly on the green velvet covered trunk like a leopard, my legs hanging down, my body horizontal, my head resting where the limb begins to curve upwards towards the light. I listened to the Coyote saying quietly: "Release your anxiety." I felt safe and I said: "I can do that!" and I let go of all the tension that I had stored in my body. It was a heavy load and, perhaps counter-intuitively, as a result my body became very heavy and sank into the tree. I had no thoughts only feelings.

Suddenly, a sensation entered my feet and an intense rush of energy streamed through me, it surged through my root centre, flooded my sexual centre, and reached my solar plexus, but the racing current had overwhelmed the sexual centre and it shattered with a feeling that was exactly like an orgasm. I was in shock but I decided: "Go with it! I am a psychological mess and I have to change." And the fact was that the energy flowing in the tree had built up in my body to such an extent that it broke through all restrictions, the dam burst. I lay without moving on the tree. I love the tree. I just love the tree. So now, I am in love with a tree!

As I lay there, my thinking capacity slowly returned, and I decided to try again to sink into the tree to see if the force could indeed flow on, beyond the solar plexus, right through me. The experience was less intense, but the flow did course right up my body, without encountering further obstacles, and out through the top of my head.

It came to me that trees don't turn off, they are on all the time; they are open channels of energy. I lay thinking about it and I decided that if my energy centres are blocked, turned off, or disabled by my choice, then the power can't flow through and that puts me in isolation, so I should work to clear them, even if, as the spirits just showed me, it means using high explosives.

The tree by the running water is a highly charged place, and I felt highly charged. I thanked the tree, thanked the energy. I'll press on and see what happens. Inching cautiously forwards in such unknown realms, and always checking my integrity, I will watch carefully for any unhelpful results. I have to think and think and think, or maybe, I should just stop 'thinking' about it.

green velvet

Two days later, I woke up and lay in bed with my arms flung out, asymmetrical, and feeling very weird. I pulled myself together physically, in a line, with my arms straight and lying against my body on either side. This enabled everything to come into line for the meditation and the spirit body started to move. This straight line technique developed from an insight that came to me in the wood and it contains an essential thought about energy. If you have understood about the energy of the tree and have experienced the power of that energy and know the strength of the tree and appreciate the simplicity of the shape of the tree, the column, then, when you copy that, the energy will flow straight, strong and true.

It is a Sunday, and I nearly didn't travel today. I thought I would opt instead for a short meditation and then go out walking, but something suggested: "No, stick to the hour." I am glad I did. On entering into the meditative state, I found that I could float and I floated into the air. I looked down at the forest, absorbing the energy that was rising from it, and I realized that I could enter the spirit circle by means of the exhalations of the trees. The trip began.

The Coyote and I were walking on the Fell and he was explaining to me that physical sex had nothing to do with the force of the tree acting on the sexual centre, the centre of generation, as I could clearly understand if I thought about the differences. And he suggested I should explore that until I understood it well. We were halfway between the green velvet Tree of Water and the heart-shaped Tree of Earth. The feeling was numinous in the extreme: I knew I had moved from my own small mind. I stood absorbing the feeling of the power for a while, learning to perceive it and learning to allow myself to receive it, and then we walked on to the tree of the heart. I looked at the triangular-shaped trunk and on the ground in front of it the corresponding triangle, the patch of grass, and I laid myself down there again.

This time, being in the meditative state, I did not resist. The Coyote and the two guides in human form, the Grandfather and the Medicine Man, pushed me into the ground and we went down under the tree into a wonderful place: a great luminous, cavernous place, the colour grey predominating but light enough to see all round, not at all like being underground. As I stood there, I noticed the three guides moving farther and farther away. They were watching, but I was on my own. What happened next was up to me, and I wanted to look around.

I began to look around, trying, by turning my head, for an all-round view, something I thought I should be able to do in the spirit body. I couldn't do it but there is a creature that can do it, that can turn its head through one hundred and eighty degrees in each direction, the Owl. The Tawny Owl came and I went into the spirit of the Owl.

tawny owl

Turning our head to the left, we took off and flew. We flew under the Fell through the grey light. I felt myself changing radically and we went through into yet another world, landing on a rock. We stood on this rock for a time, the Owl becoming in me, me becoming in the Owl.

There was an extensive preening of feathers, followed by a ruffling of feathers to test their condition. There was a period of motionless sitting, of listening with exquisite hidden ears. There was the scratching of a sudden itch followed by the sound of claws tinging on the rock. There was a slow blink as nictitating membranes slid across the surface of the dark eyes, which, as the head swivelled in each direction, stared penetratingly at the passing all-round view. Many experiences came together and made it possible for me to know how to become the Owl.

Taking off again, I flew in the sky of that world, in shades of blue, salmon pink, and yellow. It was so enjoyable. Gliding down an abyss, I landed on a tree that had grown and died on the cliff face. I surveyed the ground many miles below, looking to see what I could bring back. I saw a little black square, a lorry, travelling along a motorway with millions of others, looking like an ant. I swooped down to get it, and, as my talons gripped the black box, I knew that within was the entrance to many worlds.

I did not want to leave this adventure and it was with reluctance that I flew back to where the guides were waiting under the tree, but when I saw the three of them I was very happy, they were so strong. Suddenly I felt very weak because I must have lost the bird's body now and I was falling down. They gathered around me. My face was towards the Coyote, I put my head on his shoulder while the other two supported me on either side, and I fainted there into their strength and they strengthened me. I could see them better than before, more solid, with less fuzzy outlines, but I was in a devastated state, incapable of my own will. They picked me up and they carried me. They took a very long route down to the bottom of the tree world and round the landscape from the west to the north to the east, singing and chanting. I don't think even they exactly knew how it was going to work out, but they seemed to be able to take appropriate steps as they tried things and moved the process along.

How did I get back to my everyday self? I sat up and flexed

my spine. I felt terrible, yes, I felt terrible, like I could throw up. I felt my travelling body coming back into my physical body; that's what caused me to be a bit sick. Nevertheless, I enjoyed the returning feel of my physical body, and so, to return completely, I rubbed it with my hands, but I still feel ill and it may very well be that, even doing that, I didn't quite get back.

I am going to try an experiment. I am going to try speaking and recording as I am experiencing. There may be a lot of silence, but I will begin:

"My mind and my body are rising now. I feel undulations deep in the back of my head, low down at the base of the skull. In front of the spinal column, I feel very full of activity. I am aware of my feet in spiritual terms, just by thinking they can be a thousand miles away. As I travel up my body my anxiousness, my alertness, may hit the energy centres as I come up. They are like wells or springs, feeding pools of energy. Today my centre of generation is pulling inwards, reducing, shrinking in on itself. My hands, especially the tips of my fingers, are extending. From my elbows tension flows into my solar plexus, disappears there as black and yellow spokes, but the black centre is what draws my attention, I can feel my tension disappearing there in the timeless moment. Yes, the bottom of my body is built now and I'm breathing deeply through my solar plexus. Just now the right side of my head pulsated, affecting the left side of my heart and my knees, all exploded in purple lights and I was in my head looking down into my heart which is green and calm and full, a silver ring around it. Looking into my seeing eye now, seeing this difference: the centres lower down in my body, I feel rooted in them, up here in the higher ones I feel more detached. All I can see of the throat today is blue sky. I can feel myself rising upwards into this sky, rising upwards at the shoulders. Ah....... Eh........ My hands have completely disappeared now."

I travelled to the eye centre where I connected to the Owl, and, finally, up to the centre at the top of the head, where I became fully aware that everything was in balance and worked together, no parts were causing problems like they do when they are out of sync. Hoping to bring this awareness with me, I felt I should come back. I called and I asked: "Coyote help me so I can return." For a while nothing happened except that the left side of my head was all prickly and pulsing. I didn't fight it; I accepted it. Suddenly there was a swoosh and all the buzzing went away, and here I am ready for breakfast.

So I came back by asking for help and then waiting in a state of detachment until the process was done. This is infinitely the best way to return but sometimes I am not able to achieve this surrender. The passage above, enclosed in inverted commas, is, except for the absence of the periods of silence, exactly what was on the tape. It is the only example I recorded describing the altered state experience as it happened. As a rule, the recording was done in a halfway state, suspended between where I had been and where I would soon be, in a place of recall and record; the place I had just left was the universe within my Being and the place I was going to be in soon was the realm of daily life. One was seamless; the other had yet to be sewn together, an apt metaphor for someone who earns their living as a seamstress.

Two days later, when I woke up, I noticed a bad feeling in my solar plexus. I tried to discover what it was about as it was blocking the inflow of spiritual feelings. I remembered how deeply content and happy I had briefly been after the experience with the green velvet Ash tree and then, because it had been so unexpected, so unknown and so powerful, how I had gradually become freaked out and confused with worries, such as: "Might I get lost and go the wrong way?" Well, nothing to lose, I was already lost.

When I came to meditate, I lay quietly. I soon realized that I should go to that tree. I wanted to go to that tree; there was no problem with that, and I set out. I visualized the space made by the branches, the space within the shade of the canopy, the safe place created there. I created the gulley, I created the space, I created the sensation of safety, and I sat on the horizontal trunk. I understood how the spiritual force running free in nature co-operated with me, a house-dwelling human Being, because I went out and stumbled across it and lined myself up with it. It had created a safe place for my exploration and I deeply needed the safety of it.

When I reached a state of surrender I entered, letting the weight of my relaxed body take me in, embracing the feelings it brought me. It was enjoyable. It was wonderful. I allowed myself to flow and I became very strong. I became the trunk and branches and my root centre went out into the ground with the roots of the tree. This was an extraordinarily powerful feeling. With my Being rooted in the ground I just got stronger and stronger. I thought of myself more and more as the bark surrounding the heartwood. All the ground energy was locked into my Being, rising up inside me.

Eventually I came back. I didn't quite know where I was. My body had gone very lightweight; it was undulating. I ran my hands all over my body to get back the feeling of it. It's a nice shape; it's smooth, a bit like a sculpted container. A delicious feeling came over me and I heard this: "I found a place of safety and from this place my spirit body can walk."

Now, at last, it was time to be with my Teacher again and I travelled north to attend a seminar at Newbold House, Forres, where, once a year at that time, he and the leader of the healing group ran a seminar together.

I arrived, the day before the course started, in time for the overtone chanting that my Teacher led in a turf-roofed chamber on the Foundation called the Nature sanctuary. During the opening singing, the sounds of the overtones created waves that moved out into the surrounding darkness; undulating and rippling they were audible for a very long time and resonated with such intensity that they became embedded in me. Later that night I was able to connect to them again and it seemed that they were causing my spirit body to break up. The bottom half below the rib cage moved dramatically to the left and the top to the right. Like the ground in an earthquake, cracks opened, the land fell away, and I saw amazing new types of scenery appearing; watching them, I must have gone to sleep.

The next morning I woke up to meditate. Again, it was like the left side of my body was rapidly falling away. In contrast, the right side was immobile and solid. It was unnerving; I was in many places at once. I was in all directions. I didn't know where to settle, where to rest.

Words came to me: "Go to the Ash tree by the water." The Ash tree? But, before I had time to think about it further, there I was, right inside the main trunk. The outer ring of the limb formed a container for my energy. This was the best place to be, held there I could define my energy fields without being scattered in all directions. As I meditated, I felt the spiritual force of the ground come in from the root up. When it got to my chest level there was a change in the way that the arrangement worked and I became the rim of the branch containing the energy within.

The seminar is big, eighteen, including the two leaders. The people are very diverse. A red cloth, laid in the centre of the circle, is the medicine altar; I had brought the wings and tail of the treecreeper with me and I put them in the eastern quarter. I saw myself as a treecreeper, a tiny bird clinging to the tree and living off its bounty. Cleaning away parasites, I could see that as my job.

It was time for the first drum journey of the seminar. As we prepared, I glanced at the medicine cloth. I felt the subtle colours of the tree-bark design on the wings of the Treecreeper enter my consciousness in a special way.

The opening instruction for the journey was: "Go to a favourite place in nature and wait." The drumming started. Immediately I heard the impact of the bird on the glass. It lay dead on the pavement below my window. I was in it and it was in me. Dead on the pavement on the main street through the village, this was hardly a favourite place in nature.

The bird and I resurrected ourselves by travelling back through time. We rose up to the window pane and, travelling in reverse, went backwards, way back, through the yew tree across the road, and way, way back, back to the Ash tree in the gulley on the Fell. We landed high on the branch that grows out over the water. I clung to the bark, like a Treecreeper does, and began to search for insects lurking below.

The first insect I ate was the Coyote. I saw a flash of yellow as he disappeared. I saw him, a split second later I swallowed him. I thought: "Oh dear, I didn't even greet him." It would be complicated now he was inside me and, in order to meet him, I had to invert myself by going in through my own mouth and down into my own body. I entered. My blood vessels, capillaries and corpuscles were like branches, twigs, and leaves. I met the Coyote in the canopy of the tree. Beyond the branches of the tree, there was darkness; he was going in that direction, upwards.

We broke out into the blackness and we played. We ran about and jumped up and down and never ran into any boundaries. I investigated, and I found that the edges of the blackness were flexible and invisible. There were boundaries, but, no matter how acrobatic I became, I never ran into them.

The next day we listened to a tape of Joseph Rael, visionary and mystic, singing the sound of water. First, I felt all my energy of moving forwards sucked out through my back, a strange feeling. I must have resisted because I heard someone gently saying: "Let the flow go backwards" and then I flowed out, melting into a running stream, not fast and turbulent but clear and sparkling, light reflecting. The stream flowed down my body and entered into my generative centre. The water collected there in a deep pool; the sound of water had taken me to the centre of generation.

After a few weeks back at home, I was none too happy when I woke up and saw how good the weather was that day; I really wanted to go out on my own and I was afraid I would get stopped by something from my everyday life. But, as it worked out, I was on the Fell all day. The weather was perfection; the intense heat from the sun had dried and warmed the ground. I walked up the flowing river to the place where, with the help of the waterfall, I sing.

My centre of generation was quiet and my solar plexus was active. I was at the oak tree bend in the river looking at a tree growing in the steep ravine on the opposite bank, marvelling at its tenacity, when a bird landed in that tree with a loud squawk. I saw flashes of red, black and white plumage. When it settled on the trunk, I saw that it was a great spotted woodpecker. It had a mate and soon they were jumping noisily around the tree, ripping insects out from under the bark. There were bits of bark flying everywhere.

I moved along to the singing place and sang the vowel sounds; as I sang I looked outwards, watched the scenery, and disappeared into nature in that way. I watched the crows and rooks and jackdaws; there was a huge tribe of them, all three species mixed in together, doing aerobatics in the gulley; all landing on a particular tree very close to me and then flying up in unison and sailing on the breeze as if they were celebrating something, the good weather probably. It was wonderful to watch this while I was singing, wonderful to watch the black birds against the blue sky with the golden sun behind. I feel a strong connection with my Teacher, which is good, may I stay happy!

The beautiful image I saw, in the worlds within, was of a great tree full of light against a blue sky, the indentations on the lovely brown crinkly bark were highlighted by the angle of the light. This vision brought to my mind thoughts about the birds that have lately visited me: the tawny owl, the treecreeper, and the woodpecker. They have medicine for me, and I saw that it would help me to be like them. I spent time discovering the different ways in which they are interdependent with the trees. For example, here is a thread: the treecreeper lives on the periphery of the tree, hanging on the bark and cleaning the cracks between, roosting and nesting in the cavities. The woodpecker cleans the periphery too, but also picks insects out from further into the tree, excavating a hollow in which to roost and nest. Then the tawny owl, searching for a place to incubate her eggs, comes to that hollow and flies out from there to hunt beyond the safety of the tree.

Yesterday there was a long message on the answer phone from the leader of the healing group. Last time I saw him I had told him that I had effectively left the group because I felt unable to join in the work they are doing. They are becoming convinced that they are all members of a group re-incarnation, a group that participated in the destruction of Atlantis. Be that as it may, the focus of my life is in the Now. He said in the message: "You are so important. The things you do are unique. The knowledge you have of astral travelling and meditation, our group can use that." Hum!

This morning I was very ready to meditate and I felt the spiritual force in my head and heart. I wanted to feel it down to my feet. It was less easy for it to enter the lower areas, but it did and it filled me up. I became aware of the Great Spirit and I was full of joy. Suddenly I felt the wings of the Owl. I took off with the glorious feeling of flying. I looked up and hanging there were the keys of a big ash tree. I felt so good. This is a path I have to tread without psychic pressure from anybody. I have to be alone and develop the useful thing in me that needs to be done. Meditate, journey deeply, that is what I will do. The leader of the healing group cannot tie me up in any power trip, because I don't want it. That is the end of it.

Thick fog hung over the countryside and it was a working day, but, at two in the afternoon, I just knew I had to go out. It was my opportunity. In the deep dark fog, I walked up the river to the oak tree near the singing place. I was stunned at the difference in the landscape, now it is so wintery. Safe within my weatherproof clothing, I lay and watched the tree, barely visible through the mist, where the woodpeckers had fed; there was no activity there, all was quiet and still. I closed my eyes and meditated for a while. When I opened them, a tiny bird was caring for the tree. It was a treecreeper. At that moment, I preferred this inconspicuous bird to the noisy woodpecker. I wondered if I have been a woodpecker but now I am going to change because I can't put the world back together when I have pecked it apart. Briefly, the clouds cleared and the sun came out.

Then I went to the Ash tree over the water, and this time I did cut back the ivy because I have decided that the ivy should not be allow to encroach on the tree further while I am around. I felt huge love for the tree. I sat there and it seemed necessary to express my love for the ground and the trees. I did this; it was my affirmation that I am made of the earth.

The next afternoon, on the way back from town, I decided to visit the Apple tree. I parked the car and entered the wood. When I walked past the place where some little saplings grow, I felt that they recognized me. I felt the whole wood recognized me and welcomed me. Close to tears, I stood there and tried to connect with whatever consciousness it was that knew I came there. While doing this, I acknowledged that, at times, the Apple tree makes me nervous, especially in the winter. To discover the cause of this I stood before it and looked, and walked round it and looked, and looked and looked at it, trying to get to its essence.

The following morning the temptation to fall away after meditating into some unconscious nirvana of painless peace was intense and the Coyote said: "Make the effort to bring the journey back. You are one of the people who can do it." That gave me the energy to do it, and so I have.

I felt very good at the beginning and met the Coyote in a greater mind than mine, I feel. The thing was to stay there. I thought that was going to be fairly easy, but a huge force came rushing down from above, not golden, not beautiful, but dark and turbulent, and I was tempted to go with it like a leaf on a river. I mean, it wasn't just tempting, it was very probable; I had nothing to hang on to and the Coyote seemed to have disappeared. I couldn't get any help and, while I tried to stay in the same place, the current was rushing past me. When the experience stopped, I was disorientated and not where I had been before. I had to struggle to get back there and that was hard, but I managed to re-connect with the Coyote in the greater mind, and he brought in the beautiful colour blue.

I was in the colour blue when the Apple tree appeared. In the meditative state there was a possibility that whatever I had perceived yesterday, when at the tree in the consciousness of the world of every day, would come out more strongly. And the tree had changed. It was less solid, I saw the power running within, and I saw the cellular structure of it. I mean, that I saw how it hung together as a viewable form and how, despite the fact that trees appear so solid and tough, that form is tenuous. In the greater mind it appeared as an energetic accretion which made something with a consciousness. Yes, because it held its form, it had a consciousness.

When the meditation was over and I was back, I shut my eyes for a minute, just to recover, and I saw a picture of four huge Trees planted in a square. With their straight brown branch-free round trunks they were like gigantic Fir Trees. In the centre of the square, there was a sacred space; I was so intrigued and tempted by the very different atmosphere there that I entered that space. I looked up and a similar Tree was hovering in the air above me. It had no roots in the ground: the trunk had been sliced through horizontally. The base was flat and I could see the heartwood. My impulse was to lie beneath it: "Madness! Madness, if it comes down it will kill me stone dead." Nevertheless, I placed my generative centre right below that Tree. The result was stunning. My centre of generation started to click loudly. There was an energy exchange; the vibrations of the Tree, particularly from the outer rim, opened my generative centre up and the yellow heartwood became its centre. The feeling was absolutely brilliant: "I wonder what it means?" I had no idea, but at least, even if I did not know what the significance could be, the imagery was comprehensible.

It is Christmas day, and this morning I went for a walk up past the last farm in the village, along the top fields, and into the bluebell wood. I noticed immediately how meditative the landscape was, how the atmosphere changed me, how I entered a different mood, and that was really good. I went to visit the silver birch tree I love, the place was very open and clear and uplifting, I lay down. The wind was strong. The tree tops were swaying and, looking up at the black twigs against the grey sky, the light was very bright, almost too bright to look at.

I shut my eyes and listened to the wind causing the trees to roar. As I lay there I felt my spinal column undulate, the ground was moving beneath me. I realized that I was lying directly along the line of a root of the tree I was lying beneath. I often lay here and, without knowing it, I had always lain along the line of this root, which ran near to the surface of the earth as birch roots do. When the wind moved the top of the tree, the movement came all the way down the trunk and rippled the ground where the roots ran. It was really novel to feel the ground move in response to the wind. It was mind-altering because it felt just like a spiritual movement of the spine, and I lay against the root as it ran away into the ground and I ran with it.

I was very pleased at this point because, in the wood, I am able to do a meditative journey in a way that I like. Which is that I manage to reach a state of mind where, if I want to, I can say: "Stop!" and I can stop, store what has happened in my memory, and go on from the stopping point without losing the thread. I thought of how often the Coyote has helped me to remember and how he has awakened these techniques. I called to him and he suggested: "Let's join our energy centres together." I was pleased to do this. As we came together in each centre, the pictures happened. The images were like food, and I saw.

In the root centre, I saw a dish with a mound of black soil; in the generative centre, a bowl of water; in the solar plexus, a bowl of fire; in the heart, a bowl of light. Lastly, in the throat centre I saw a bowl of air. This meditation all took place in the wood with the sound of the wind in the trees. That sound certainly helped me, like the drumming does on the journeys during seminars.

Tomorrow there is a storm wind forecast and I wonder if any of the trees that I love will be damaged, I hope not. Thank you, Coyote, for a very nourishing Christmas meal!

Year Three

The new year had begun. I lay connected to the Coyote. I felt pain in my solar plexus, desire, longing, and he said: "Feel it! Express it!" I did and the medicine wheel colours came; white first, and then came black, then red, then yellow. The colours became a long dark tunnel. With no ability to be mobile from my own mind because I didn't know where I was or what I was doing, I fought my way along that tunnel, pushing myself, dragging myself, going onward, onward, onward.

Eventually I arrived where there was only the colour yellow. I put my forehead against it and everything in my centre of seeing went yellow. I put my heart against it and everything in my heart went yellow. I put my centre of generation against it and everything in my generative centre went yellow. I concluded: "This is a door and this is right, because yellow is the colour vibration that ushers you into the medicine wheel of life." I determined to go through this doorway, but I needed to check with the Coyote to see if that was ok. It was ok, but first he speared me with two fine wires that came through my back at my shoulder blades, looped down, went back into my body through my ribs, and out to the back again. Like a harness, he tied those into me, and I went forward into an empty space filled with a greyish, yellowish half-light, something like a huge stone room.

I lay down there and after a little while I felt an adrenaline thrill which, perhaps, ran from above my heart down to the level of my centre of generation but I didn't seem to have those things any more. I had a spinal column and the thrill took place to the left of that. It was a thrill of fear and the Coyote advised: "Don't let that fear put you off. Go for it, enter it." I entered.

I was looking into the future and the colours were black and green. I spent a long time consolidating what the future felt like, and from there I rose up into another level, the details of which I have forgotten, maybe it was further into the future. Various things happened in there, deep breathing, a few noises, and some knowledge. I half returned and opened my eyes. The Coyote drew out the wires and it was painful. I was back.

Oh, I lost all the section with the tree. Hopeless, forgetful woman! After I entered the second level, I realized that it was a place for dancing. The ground was black. I was green. I was the green grass of a dancing floor. I heard Joseph's voice saying: "You may be the dancing floor but first you must dance your own dance." So what would I dance? .... I would dance like the trees dance in the wind, when the roots move underground to the rhythm of the sky. I sent my roots down, down into the ground to play and to dance. I sent those roots down into the earth and then I concentrated my attention where the trunk enters the ground and that was like a spinning vortex that spiralled downwards. The column, the still, the contained, part of the tree rose upwards, on, up into the branches, into the great head, which was, to my mind at that time, only moved by the wind. Animals came and played in the tree; that was part of the dance as well. I danced in my roots, my mind was danced upon, and my body connected roots and mind. So that was my dance, it made me laugh because my dance was a tree. I thought happily: "One day I will tell people how to dance like trees."

When dusting the bookshelf, the day before yesterday, I came across a slim book, printed on fine quality paper with hand-cut pages. It had belonged to my Grandmother. The book is called *On the Beautiful;* an english translation of the ideas of a graeco-egyptian mystic called Plotinus. I thought: "Yes, at that time the mystical philosophers were developing abstract thought. Most people then lived in the natural world and it was time to connect to the world of ideas so he wrote *On the Beautiful.* Now, many people live in the world of ideas and maybe the Coyote and I will write *On Trees* to help people connect mystically back into the world of nature again." It was an appealing idea.

inside the hollow tree

This morning, as I entered the meditative trance, I spent a long time entering the body of the Owl and I had discomfort in my solar plexus. After a while, I began to breathe deeply, making noises like the rushing sound of air blowing through a hollow pipe. After a great deal of effort I turned these sounds into the vowel sound -uu, which is the sound of carrying, and I sang out loud: "-uu" listening, as my Teacher has suggested, to the silence afterwards, something that I am not very accomplished at, listening to the silence, that is.

The pain in the solar plexus went away. I was perched on a totem pole, maybe it was a personal totem pole, but it certainly was a totem pole, very, very tall, and I perched on it with my wings outstretched, then I folded them and settled down. Sat up there I remembered that I could, by turning my head one hundred and eighty degrees in each direction, see all round. I turned my head to the right. At the halfway point, looking down to the ground so far below, I saw distant tipis. Turning to the back, I saw golden pyramids. They glittered, attracting my attention, and I gazed at them for some time. I turned my head to the front again and realized that I had been looking into the past. To the left was the future, and there were also two parts to it. The first part I really wanted, the second part was a different thing, and I wanted the first part. The Coyote said: "Go get it." I flew down to pick it up. It was a package, as I gripped it a talon pierced the wrapping, through the tear I glimpsed blue inside, perfect blue. I brought it back to the top of the pole and placed it in my heart. I settled down, waiting.

After a while, the Coyote came into my centre of seeing. We joined there, so perfect, no fizzing around the edges where the contact wasn't complete; it was complete. It was beautiful, no question of who was which because we were one and ourselves. Eventually the experience faded, my eyes opened and I came back here.

When I looked out of the window, the quality of the light was pink. The sky is still grey, as it has been for days and days and days, but the light quality at that moment was pink, some effect of the hidden sunrise. It has gone now, but it was so lovely to see because it was the complimentary colour to the blue, which I had placed in my heart. All I saw of my future package, on this occasion, was clear blue light and I was content with that. That would be something! To join the blue light, that would be something!

It was mid March when I next worked with my Teacher in a seminar setting. The time came to take a drum journey to the middle world, always a difficult, confusing place for me. The instructions were: "Go to an island, the power animal will join you, travel through the mist together and see what happens."

I saw a landscape, rugged and wild. A shallow rock-strewn river ran through it. No boat could navigate those waters and there was no island. I saw a log stranded on the rocks. Perhaps it was a dugout canoe. But, no, it was a large piece of the trunk of a tree. Too curious I got trapped inside. A great flood came and swept the fallen tree down the river, leaving it high and dry on an island.

I was trapped inside. How could I possibly get out? I heard something, a loud knocking on the outside of the trunk; a Woodpecker was there, hammering his way into the wood. By his efforts he rapidly split the trunk and I was able to emerge. At the sight of me, the bright feathers of his red cap rose up in a magnificent display before slowly subsiding to their former sleekness. I thanked him profoundly for releasing me and decided to journey with him. We were about to fly off when I realised: "Wait a minute there's something wrong, we haven't done the mist." He dismissed the idea of mist, with a: "Pur-pher!" and the little mist that was knocking about, waiting for its opportunity, vanished in the face of his impatience.

Travelling fast, we headed in a northerly direction. I felt I must speak again: "Hold on, if we go too far north there won't be any trees for you to bore holes in." At the very edge of the tree line we landed.

great spotted woodpecker

I had been flying behind him, and, all the way through the flight, I had been fascinated by the bright red cap on his head. Landing in this patch of vibrant colour, I rummaged around at the base of the red feathers where they enter the skin on the skull. I was thinking:

"This is insane. What am I doing?" But my thoughts didn't stop me, and slowly I sank into the Woodpecker's head, then down into the body, where, unaccountably, the body of the Woodpecker became a tree and I was trapped again. I thought: "The only difference in this state to the one I was in previously is that I am now stuck vertically instead of horizontally. How am I going to get out now? Will I have to stay here for the rest of this journey?" It seemed a distinct possibility.

The Coyote arrived outside, and he shouted through the bark: "Make the tree flexible." It is totally unclear how but somehow this was accomplished and I was able to step down into the clearing and stand beside him. Then there was a long period when we did not move, where he showed me things and taught me things. What was he teaching? What was he doing? I can't remember: it's a blank. After a time, when he said: "Follow me" I found that I couldn't: I was stuck again.

Then, because I had lost it, he advised me, he wasn't exasperated, but, looking for the next step, he advised me to stay still, saying: "Well, you might as well relax and listen to the drum." I did, and the continuous second note that I have heard before became audible and became very, very important to me. As I listened to it, wondering how it was created, I began to rise up very slowly into a beautiful dark space. The feeling of rising was very, very enjoyable, and I lay suspended in the dark space listening to the drumming. The Coyote told me to listen to it carefully, and, as I listened, I thought: "This will heal my heart, stop the arrhythmia, and make me feel happy." The Coyote said: "Listen to the drum bringing you the sounds of the future. Listen to the drum telling you what's coming in the future. Wait, wait, wait." He wanted to impress upon me that there is nothing more I need to do now but that, so I listened to the drum and let it affect my heart and a huge spiritual healing took place. I felt it spread over me. I could feel it working in my body. I felt very grateful that this was happening; I tried to be as pliable as possible and absorb it all.

I was extremely aware of the internal world of my body and the external world of the seminar. Outside the room a large, noisy skein of geese were approaching. I heard them coming, and I thought: "Oh, here's what the future is bringing. What are the geese saying? What do they mean?" And no insights came from it, they flew right by. A little while later, a second skein went over, even noisier, and I got a feeling that I was shielded lying in the black space. A feeling that there was a protecting wall around me; as if I was in a dark sanctuary; all that jostling, all that point and counterpoint, all those interrelationships that form the dynamics of a group; none of that could get in. That was good; it need not involve me.

As I lay thinking that it was ok for me to be out of it, uninvolved, a novel thing for me, another universe began to open up on my left-hand side. It was the most fabulous semi-transparent landscape of vertical drops into a deep blue sky and vertical cliff walls with luminous plants and great trees growing on them, all illuminated by that especially clear and coolly brilliant, shining light. I have seen this place before; meditating after a perfectly ordinary walk on the Fell, re-walking the walk in my mind, I descended through the ground and discovered that this exotic and extraordinary nature world existed below. I looked down into it now. It opened from the space where I was, in the most soft way; a most inviting and seductive sensation of vertigo overtook me and I wanted to throw myself down into that fantastic world. I knew that I would not plummet down; I would float. And I knew that possibly all I could do was drift endlessly and observe it. Nevertheless, it was infinitely fascinating to me and I wanted to go.

Suddenly I heard a banging under the floorboards right by my left ear. The Coyote was knocking violently on the floorboards, but the noise wasn't in the journey it was happening in fact. The Coyote was calling me: "Come under the floor bones with me. I want you here, come under the floor bones." And I thought: "Oh no! I don't want to go under the floorboards. What's under there? What's under there but dust and spiders?" The knocking got louder and eventually, because he was calling me, I did go through the wooden boards and under the floor.

Under-there opened out into a completely different landscape, more like a landscape from our world, more like some familiar countryside laid down to green pasture lightly dotted with trees. I was looking at it, wondering if it was as interesting as that fabulously otherworldly universe that I had wanted to vertigo myself into, when the drumming changed calling us to come back.

"Oh, I don't want to leave here now. And, not only do I not want to leave here but I've no way of getting back without the Coyote." It had been so complicated: some of it was in visual pictures like a journey, some of it was spiritual healing, some of it was body shifts, some of it was here, some there, some nowhere, so I called him and he brought me back and I haven't lost much.

It was on the way back that a wind came up and disturbed the trees outside the room. I could hear them swishing and I thought: "Yes, by the power of the wind the trees are unstuck. That is how to make the tree flexible."

Occasionally when I was in a group of people working with my Teacher, he would organise a trance dance. We would go to the dance studio and dance the electronic sounds of the trance music, written by his friend, through every cell of our body. Just now, I recalled the trance dance of this seminar week and I remembered that as soon as the music began my body started to move, invoking the spirits from below to rise, rise, rise, then the spirits from above to descend, descend, descend, descend, my body remembering how it was done. When those spirits were present I danced with them in the horizontal and I danced with them in the vertical. I danced with the elements and I danced to the four directions. During a beautiful section of soaring uplifting sound I danced a dance in honour of the eagle.

Then there was a change in the music and a terrible military regime began. I danced my way through memories of several lives of war. All the time I danced these war dances I was sick of it. I hated it. I wanted to break the cycle so much. I wanted to dance out of rhythm. I wanted to smash up this regular rhythm that was militarising my existence. I became a slave. I became a captive and eventually I became somebody approaching a death that they had come to by a defeat in war. Ahead of me I saw a tall wooden pole whose diameter was slightly less than the diameter of the trunk of my body. I saw that pole with joy; I threw myself at it and smashed my Being into a thousand fragments.

During this seminar, my Teacher gave us each a precious gift, a dried leaf from a Sun Moon Dance Tree. The Sun Moon Dance is a ceremony gifted to all people by Beautiful Painted Arrow, Joseph Rael. I know very little about this dance but my Teacher goes to America to participate in it and he holds it in very high regard, and so, therefore, do I.

Back at home, meditating one day at seven in the morning, as was my practice, I shut my eyes and I was the Owl perched on top of the newel post in the yet-to-be-completed bungalow that the Coyote is renovating for me. Looking down I saw that the foot of the post was set in the centre of a circle, a circle divided into quarters. Each quarter was a different medicine wheel colour and the ground looked like a stationary spinning top. I flew down into the colour white and I was a white Owl. I crossed the division into the black, where all colours are hidden. I flew on into the red and I was a tawny Owl. Then I flew into the yellow and the Owl was the colour of honey. I returned to the top of the newel post, but, as I settled there, I was sucked down into it and I became wood. I became the post, a symbolically simple tree, and the four colours of the medicine wheel flew out of the top of this 'tree' like fountains. The bottom of the 'tree' that was buried in the ground sent out streamers that mirrored the shape above. These underground streamers were brown, like roots, and they remained brown as they penetrated the earth and returned to the surface. At ground level, the two fountains met. All below was brown and, above the ground, the post itself was brown but, from the top of it, the four colours were raining down each filling a quarter with a vibrant light: white, black, red, and yellow.

So, here I am in a caravan at the Foundation, just six weeks since I last visited and quite surprised to be here. I never expected the seminar I was travelling to on the Island of Skye to be cancelled. I expected to visit Findhorn to pick up my Teacher and take him there to lead the group. I did not expect to be here for four days. When it became clear that was going to happen I kicked myself for not having my laptop with me and the Coyote is laughing and laughing, asking me if I am freaked out to be thrown upon my own resources without technology?

On the second day in the caravan I had a bit of difficulty getting into my early morning meditation but luckily my spiritual friends were insistent. I had to overcome some problems, problems such as whether to have toast or porridge for breakfast, for instance. But very soon I felt the gentle energy of the deer and, entering my heart centre, the deer began to penetrate my Being in a way that I could not ignore. I felt my generative centre energise. Yesterday, sat out on the dunes, I felt the energy stirring but I moved away from it: travelling through time in the daily world I had become insular again and felt reluctant to connect in that way. Now I allowed the energy to awaken. I looked at the roe deer's skull that I had found half-buried in the dunes many months before, and it is strange how things, which I know perfectly well, come back at such moments so vividly that they seem brand new.

As if I had never seen them before, I noticed the antlers rising upwards and I saw that the deer skull is the shape of a heart with blood vessels branching out of it. The antlers, silhouetted against the sky, look like the branches of a tree, and, indeed, the antlered skull looks very like the tree of the heart on the Fell. I wondered: "Where are the roots of the heart?" In response, my centre of generation activated and I saw that the roots of the tree grasp the rock. The tree breaks the surface of the ground at the generative centre; the trunk grows up through the solar plexus and on, carrying the heart upwards. The spreading branches growing from the heart reach out to the upper world while the generative centre holds the heart in this world at the point where sky meets land: the heart's roots are in the earth.

I stayed with that understanding for a long time, deeply envisaging the deer as my heart's guardian, and, during this process, my ever-present sense of heartache was eased. Lying there, I noticed that the meditation had begun with diversions from the world of appetites, which threatened to deprive me of spiritual opportunities and I struggled to overcome them. When I had succeeded, I discovered that the attractions and the passions of daily life forge the connections that keep my heart here.

My Teacher felt that we hadn't quite finished the work that we were doing this weekend, work which had come about instead of going to Skye, so I stayed an extra night. Maybe this was the night that he showed me a photograph of a Sun Moon Dance Tree. It was in the shape of a Y, symbolising the two lights that support our world, and a clear memory back to experience week returned to me, where the two spirit guides, one feminine, one masculine, had descended and I had united with them in this form, a Y-shape. I was surprised to see that the diameter of the Sun Moon Tree was not very big and that it had been stripped of bark up to a certain height. It did not then look unlike the tree I smashed myself upon in the trance dance.

Soon after this, in early May, I did visit the Isle of Skye for the first time. A Sound Peace Chamber, a place for chanting ourselves into harmony as taught by Joseph Rael, had recently been built there, and I had received an invitation to go to the activation ceremony. It must have been about half past three in the morning when the ceremony finished but I was not in the slightest bit tired. All my brain circuits had been turned on and they didn't switch off now. After the others left the chamber site to go to the house, I took two willow twigs and put their ends into the ashes of the fire that, through the hours of darkness, had burned brightly outside the chamber. The willow twigs caught light and smouldered, glowing in the dark. They reminded me of the antlers of the deer and I touched my forehead with them three times. I stuck them, still smouldering, upright in the ground of the fire pit and went to my tent.

I lay there and I noticed that the ground had completely changed its angle of inclination so that I seemed to be sliding down towards my feet. This change made me feel that I must be in an altered state; when I lay in the tent the night before the ground had been horizontal. I lay on my back, thinking meditatively, when suddenly a Deer arrived, a strange otherworldly creature with big ears but no antlers, a female Deer. She had very, very large, deep-black eyes; she spoke gently: "Follow me." I thought: "I will, but shall I go consciously or unconsciously?" I felt that I couldn't make it consciously; it would be too much, so, with absolute trust, I turned over and dropped into blackness with the Deer. In the morning when I woke up, in that place between sleeping and waking, all the voices of nature sounded different to me, as if, with a little effort, I could understand their language.

The next day the chamber keepers were taking their american guests out to visit some places on the island. They invited me, but I decided not to go. I took down my tent and moved into an empty bedroom in the house. When I lay down to process the recent happenings I felt very, very ill, but when I got up, to hang out the washing and various other chores that I had undertaken to do, I felt fine. In meditation my brain felt dreadful, especially the left-hand side, maybe it was a body adjustment to the spiritual input. I knew already the kind of physical symptoms that you can get. Whatever it was, I determined to get through the process, so, without any understanding of what was going on, I stayed horizontal and began to work my way through the labyrinth.

I don't remember very much. I know that I lay there travelling for four or five hours, and at some point, in the spherical space that I was sharing with the Coyote, I saw what I thought was a lump of wood. Suddenly spirit voices said to me: "Eat the tree." And I ate it, I chewed it with my spirit body and I ate it. As I concentrated on eating, something was enabled to be done. Don't ask me what this was because I have no idea. But I distinctly remember chewing the tree, and as I ate it the Coyote came so close to me that his eyes were right up against my eyes. I felt him to be extremely real and a part of the world of everyday and it was very exciting.

When I had begun to eat the tree I had thought: "This is barmy." But still I did it. I ate it from the top down and when I reached ground level I thought: "Thank goodness, I have finished it." It was quite a chew. Then they said: "Eat the roots as well." But, in fact, the roots were more like liquid and I sucked them up until I could see that below ground where they had been there was a large hollow chamber. I blew air into this chamber and tiny fibrous hairs of the roots that were left stuck to the walls were blown off, enabling me to ingest them as well. So I consumed the entire tree. And things happened in my body which I can't explain or describe except that, for the first time, something radically shifted in my throat centre. That night I slept, it was the first night's sleep without being woken for a spiritual event that I had since I arrived on Skye.

The next day I brought the american couple, on their way to a Sound Peace Chamber in Wales, south to my house in north Yorkshire. I took them to visit the Apple tree. They did a ceremony to bless the tree and we sang. Well, they sang, but I was overwhelmed, began to weep and could not sing.

Just now I have meditated and, after searching for and seeing Joseph and also connecting strongly into the Apple tree, the memory of the devastating moment in the blue light vision, when all the trees vanished and there was only blackness, came back to me. I still don't understand it, although I seem to think that it might be something to do with the nature worlds calling out to us, humans, to become more aware.

My life of intent is nothing short of miraculous. I have been dying to go out for a walk for three days and at two o'clock today I managed to get out. I walked up the hill out of the village and along the track past the farm. I felt expectant, like I was going to witness a miracle. I looked out over the fields and I thought my whole life was a miracle. The light was exceptional. The landscape was beautiful with green grass and blue sky caring for the white sheep. I went to the bluebell wood and felt incredibly excited by the presence of the many trees.

in the bluebell wood

I glimpsed a small deer quietly jump away then I lay down in my usual place. The yellow sun was shining through the trees upon me, I saw blue sky, I saw green trees, and I saw white trunks of the birch trees patched with black and I thought about the colours of the six directions: "Blue and green are above and below, but where is the fourth colour of the cardinal directions? Where is the colour red? Is it only in the blood within my body? Is that the place that I have to imagine it because I can't see it here with my eyes open?"

I shut my eyes and I heard the whirr of the wings of a tiny bird very close to me. I opened my eyes and, on the white bark of the silver birch to my right, a treecreeper had landed only six or seven feet away. It began busily to clean the bark of the tree, and it was very wonderful to see that tiny bird alive and so close. Then I became aware of another bird, higher up in the adjacent tree. At first I assumed it was the treecreeper's mate but it was twice the size and I realized that it was a great spotted woodpecker and that the colour red had arrived on cue. Next minute the treecreeper flew from its own tree and landed beside the woodpecker as if they were looking for insects together. Then the woodpecker flew off at a tremendous rate and the treecreeper followed it. Indeed, they were working together: the woodpecker disturbing small insects which the treecreeper gleaned.

Leaving the wood, I chose a different route that took me home along the main street and I ran into the village's nosiest neighbour. "Have you been somewhere?" she asked me. "Yes, I have been out for a walk." She looked at me incredulously: "But you haven't got a dog!" I shrugged my shoulders and walked on, but in her face I glimpsed the conclusion she was drawing from this brief encounter: "She has been meeting someone in the wood!" I knew that her eyes were following me. Suddenly I was acutely aware that I had been lying in the wood wearing a fleece and that my back was probably decorated with twigs, leaves and random grasses. Her suspicions were fully confirmed and soon the whole village would know of my illicit affair and many exciting rumours would circulate wildly as to which local man it could be.

Late one night in July, my Teacher rang me from America to tell me that there is a Sun Moon Dance in Manchester at the end of the month. At the Dance he is attending in New Mexico, he has met one of the two brothers who are organising it. He gave me a telephone number to contact them if I want to go. This will be the first Sun Moon Dance in the UK and one of Joseph's close relatives will be chief. It was most exciting news. It did not take me many seconds to decide that I would dance this Dance.

After a few days, I told my partner and, when he heard that the Dance entailed refraining from food and water for several days, he was horrified and shouted at me: "You'll die! What are you doing? You don't even know these people." If I replied I do not recall it, but he was genuinely concerned and that was not the end of his attempts to dissuade me. He caused me some stress one night by coming in drunk and, with the best intentions, informing me that I was going to fail in the Sun Moon Dance because in his eyes it is some kind of an extreme encounter with fear and travelling into, what he called 'the dead zone'. Little as I know about it, it is nothing like that at all. I told him that all his military experiences were centred on fear because they did not include the spiritual dimension and that this was different in that crucial respect. He accidentally on purpose tried to demoralize me further by saying that he would come and fetch me from Manchester if I was incapacitated.

When I came to bed, I found I had the most horrible pain in my heart, like I have had once before after a psychic tussle with him. You can't call it an attack as such, it seems to be well motivated, but it is very bad news. I had to tell him to stand back and that I was going to do this on my own, an attitude that he respected. But he said that he had no faith in my Teacher and I told him, nicely, that was none of his business and he didn't have to have faith.

The next day as I drove to a customer's house I was feeling

a bit deflated and down in the dumps. As I entered the drive, a woodpecker burst out of a tree and flew low just ahead of my car all the way down the long unmade track. Its undulating flight carried it fast and effortlessly. At a flap of the wings, it rose, and, shutting the wings tight against the body, it shot, like a speeding arrow, forwards in a long low arc, until, at the bottom of the trajectory, it flapped its wings once more and rose effortlessly upwards again, so that it seemed to speed down the lane in leaps and bounds. Its mate appeared too and flew along from tree to tree. Their speed and energy and flashing colours gave me a much appreciated lift.

My Dance is a Tree

I am going to Manchester this afternoon to meet up with the people organising the Sun Moon Dance and in a day's time it will begin. I have had to witness some of my weaker points during the last few days. Maybe one of the most ridiculous was yesterday afternoon when I found myself saying to myself: "Why am I doing this? I don't even like people! I have never done anything for anybody; it is not in my nature so why am I going to participate in a ceremony to help the People?" I am just hoping this self-dissuasion will diminish as I get into the process of the Dance. But my body is not so brilliant; I feel bloated and uncomfortable, a bit sluggish and verging on fat. What a lovely description! Last night I rang my Teacher, who is still in America, to tell him I am going to dance. It was good to talk to him. After we spoke, I felt a great turmoil because I wanted to escape to the freedom and the joy that I have when working with him.

I got to Manchester just after three in the afternoon, found the flat I was looking for, and then, because I was early, I walked down the street and had a coffee. When I came back, one of the brothers was there. I had to sign a consent form that said: 'I understand fully the nature of the Dances', or something like that, so I crossed it out and wrote: 'I do not fully understand' and I signed it.

The next morning, Friday, I left Manchester early and eventually found the Dance site, which was located in the Cheshire countryside about forty minutes from the city. On a large hay field that had recently been cut, the circular arbour, made of wooden posts, was half built, and there were also two tipis spaced well apart. I decided to walk around before introducing myself to anyone. On the far side of the field, a steep incline led down to a small stream, the banks of which were a mass of willow trees mixed with other trees such as oaks and ashes. It was very pleasant to have the trees so close. The unmade road that led to the field also led to a fishing lake a little distance off, and on that side of the field there was one lone magnificent oak tree. Admiring its beauty, I walked close to it, passing underneath the lower branches just above my head, and then on to the tipi where there seemed to be the most activity. Someone handed me a cup of tea and I began to meet the people.

After a while, the Chief arrived. We all set to work finishing the arbour. When all the wooden poles were in place, we covered the sleeping places with tarpaulins. We dug the circular hole in the centre for the Tree. It was four foot deep and about two foot wide. Although I didn't do much of the digging, I really enjoyed the process of preparing the ground. We had something to eat and then it was time to go and get the Tree.

The Tree had already been chosen. I was glad to see that it was one trunk of a polled willow tree, which meant that when we took it the tree would not die, it would just give up one of its limbs. We sang and prepared to cut it. Although there was a chain saw, the Chief announced that we were going to cut it down with an axe, and this is what we did. But before the axe touched the Tree I began to weep silent, copious tears. An experienced woman said: "This is not about the Tree being killed. It is chosen to represent the World Tree. There is no reason to be sad." She did not address this directly to me, but I expect she meant it for me. There was no way and no point in explaining to her that my overwhelming sadness did not come from the tree being chopped down, it just came from trees and got me every now and again. This was one of those occasions and the cause was incomprehensible to me.

We, the dancers, carried the Tree back up to the field. I say 'we', but I was too short and really didn't carry any weight. I was glad about this. I felt none too strong. When the Tree did touch my shoulder, it felt so heavy I seemed to buckle at the knees. We laid it down outside the arbour and everyone helped to prepare it. The lower half was stripped of bark, and all the sharp points removed from this section, the scars were sealed and blackened with charcoal. Most of the branches were cut from the upper section. This left a single trunk that split into two branches about four fifths of the way up, making a Y-shape. Leaf bundles were prepared and tied to the arms of the Y. A buffalo skull was brought out of the medicine tipi and tied onto the Tree at the fork. An eagle feather was hung on each horn. Tobacco offerings wrapped in long strips of cloth, one for each of the four medicine wheel colours, were tied to the tops of the two arms of the Y, looking at the Tree from outside the east gate of the arbour, the black and white to the left, the red and yellow to the right. Another set of coloured cotton strips were tied round the point where the stripped trunk met the bark, in ascending order: yellow, white, black, and red. When all was ready, we carried the Tree into the arbour, raised and slid it into the hole with the aid of steadying ropes; it went in perfectly. The hole was slowly filled with loose soil tamped down until the Tree stood firm.

the dance tree

Now the dancers should choose their places and bring what they needed into the arbour. I was completely at a loss. What did I need? I didn't have a clue what would happen next. I didn't even know how long we would be there, or how the ceremony would proceed. I chose the space next to where the drum would be, next to the east gate. This meant that I was in the south east. I put on my sweat lodge shift and brought a sleeping mat, a sleeping bag, my poncho blanket, dance dress, kitchen roll, spare pair of knickers, and a towel. That was it, except for the small leather bag I had made and painted with the heart symbol, a circle with a vertical dividing line, one hemisphere painted yellow and the other black, which was hung round my neck. The bag hung empty until two women handed each dancer a turkey bone whistle, mine fitted neatly into the bag. "But what is it for?" I wondered.

The fire, heating the sweat lodge stones, had been burning for some hours and now we went into the lodge. It was dusk. After the sweat, a drink of water was offered and slices of watermelon were passed around, the melon tasted exquisitely delicious. This was our last food and drink.

It was time to enter the arbour. We changed into our dance clothes and donned white sheets. We danced round the outside of the arbour four times blowing the whistles and offering maize blessings to each of the directions. I found myself in a very jovial mood. Inside, I was grinning and hooting with laughter. We all looked ridiculous. To my ears, the noise the whistles made was strident and dissonant. I felt I was participating in some crazy joke. I didn't mind being involved, it was fun, but at the same time, was it serious?

We went in to our places. The Chief addressed us all and told us that whatever we had done, whether we knew what it was or not, we should forgive ourselves. I knew I was going to have trouble with this. Sure enough, during the night I wrestled with the concept of forgiveness. I found that I could not forgive myself. I couldn't just say to myself: "I forgive you." It was not enough. I had to do something, rectify something. I knew that my greater self had no lack of forgiveness, in fact, it did not judge, but I could not grant myself forgiveness here, my small self could not forgive myself. At some point I came to terms with the fact that I could not follow the Chief's instruction on this. I was not into forgiveness; I was into doing something to set matters straight.

When I began to get ill, I did wonder if my inability to forgive myself catapulted me into sickness. But before the pain started I was already quite fearful about my energy levels and I had another fear as well, which was about possession, a fear that the spiritual energy was going to come and grab me, extinguish my free will, and somehow I would be lost.

Maybe in the second dance of Saturday morning, a communication came through the Tree. It said: "You come of your own free will. There is no compulsion here. If you are called, it is your choice to come to the Tree." Hearing that made me feel much better, after that I felt that if the opportunity came, and it wasn't absolutely sure that the Tree would call me, but if it did, I had the choice as to whether I went or not and that made a huge difference to me at that moment. Now I could dance and not be held back by fear.

Then the journey started. I didn't understand it at the time, but now it seems to me to have been a rapid journey through all the surrounding levels of the astral plains into the clearer spiritual worlds, and that it was necessary so that I could find purity in order to hear spiritually while being completely conscious in this world of the Earth. A purifying of my body, so that on Sunday I could dance truly for the good of all. That seems to me to be what Saturday was about, because most of that day I was semi-conscious, especially in the time between the dance rounds.

I don't remember how the illness started, but I found my solar plexus to be knotting up and a headache to be hovering. Sometime in the morning, at the end of a dance round, I was very violently sick. The energy rush came from very low down, below my diaphragm, and the spew was white foam, nothing but white foam.

Oh, the last thing I needed was to lose fluid like this! I tried to lie on my back and meditate but this caused severe pain in my solar plexus so I lay in a heap and experienced some strange things. At the end of the following two dances, I threw up again. In among all this, there were at least three experiences of travelling at speed along a road in a car being driven by another person. The car was going so fast, it was making me sick; the blurred landscape flashing by and the swerving motion of the car were making me sick. The headache became more and more terrible and there was a constant involvement on the astral plain. Conversations with people I had never seen before, pointless and inane, involvement in processes belonging to spirits there that had nothing to do with me. I could clearly recognise this at the time but I could do nothing about it. The spirits kept bringing me drinks and food. I saw jugs of water and plates of delicious food clearly and often during the afternoon. I don't remember drinking or eating them, but contrary to what I thought would happen, I became neither thirsty nor hungry. Among all this I would hear snatches of the Dance songs and I hung onto them for dear life.

 Then there was the possibility that I had heat stroke. The symptoms I was having were very similar to the symptoms I had in Italy when I threw up in the cave of the Sibyl at Cumae. I remembered how my partner looked after me, booked us into a hotel, dunked me in a cold shower, and then sat with me all night while I slept it off. What I was experiencing physically now was so similar it brought back how caring he had been of me then. There were some attendants in the arbour called Moon Mothers, but I did not understand their role and, because I got up to dance each round and threw up in the rest periods, they didn't yet know I was in trouble and I thought: "Nobody is caring for me now. Maybe I will get delirious." Then I thought: "But these people are from a hot country and they must know the symptoms of heat stroke and they will not let me get that sick. Oh well, if I die, I die!" I was feeling rather dramatic, but it was also dawning on me that this sickness had spirit visions with it and seemed to be part of a process and that made it different to the italian illness. And, how could I get severe heat stroke in two hours on a slightly warmer than average but hardly hot english summer day?

In the middle of all that terrible turmoil, I was seriously wondering if I would be able to stay in the Dance. I saw clearly that I would not be able to tolerate the rest of my life if I didn't make it through and yet it seemed that my body was conking out. In the depths of this battle I heard a quiet voice that was my Teacher, and, behind him, his Teacher, Joseph, and beyond them another voice, like echoes of each other. I heard two words spoken in a serious and encouraging tone: "Come on!"

The Chief walked past and I told him I was being sick. He said: "That happens sometimes." I nodded: "Oh, I thought it was probably ok." He sent one of the Moon Mothers to me. I lay with my head in her lap and she soothed me. She suggested that the headache might be caffeine toxin. I wondered how she knew I drank too much coffee, especially the day before. I thanked her for looking after me and I called her 'Mother'. To my surprise I found this very easy and I remembered what a mother was.

A few rounds later, I realized that I wasn't going to make it to the end of that round before I was sick. I went back to my place and threw up. She came to me and I said: "This feels like heat stroke. I had it once in Italy." She said that it was very likely spiritual heat. I told her of the rapid car journeys and she said: "This is the fast road to the spirit." She proved her point by touching me, at a certain point on my back, between my shoulder blades with her bird's wing fan. To my surprise, I threw up immediately. She told me that I could quit, nobody would think any the worse of me. I said: "I can quit without dishonouring everybody?" She said: "Of course you can. You can quit anytime. You have done far more than I expected you to." I asked her: "Doesn't it matter if I fall down during the dancing?" I had this idea that if you fell, you dishonoured everybody. I don't know where I got that from, some book probably. Apparently, this is a less austere world. I felt some relief that I would not let people down. However, expectations from other people might be less: but what would I think of myself?

At the mid day point the Chief had said to us that the Tree might call us at any time from that point on. I said to the Moon Mother in some anguish: "The Tree is not speaking to me at all!" She said: "I am not surprised, you're too busy detoxifying." She also pointed out that other people were beating a clear path to and from the Tree while my path was just a mess. I had already noticed this. She asked me if I had wandered a lot in my life. Too sick to put up a spirited defence, I replied weakly: "I thought there was a reason for it, now I am not so sure." I had been thinking that the reason, for my long journey away from spiritual connection and my return, was to bring me to this ceremony with the right attitude, but at that moment, it looked as if I wasn't going to make it. Then my journey would all have been for nothing.

I did not get up for the beginning of the next dance, but it was not very long before the drum energised me enough to rise and join the other dancers. Despite the headache, I danced the rest of the day. It diminished when I danced and returned with a vengeance during the rest periods. To my surprise, last thing at night the Moon Mothers brought us a very small drink of medicine tea, just a couple of mouthfuls. It tasted ok. Before settling for the night, I threw up dramatically one more time, losing the precious tea. I went to sleep thinking: "How long can this go on?" I think I was sick six times altogether. It makes a good metaphor anyway, once for each direction.

When I took off my dress to get into my sleeping bag I noticed that I had been wearing it back to front all day. I could hardly believe this, especially as the embroidery on the front is so distinctive. What a completely disorientated idiot I was.

I slept deeply. I woke early and saw the Tree in the pre-dawn light. It looked so wonderful, numinous and charged with energy that it made a deep impression on me. When we got up to sing to the sunrise I felt I might be better. The Chief came and asked me how I was. "Better, I think, better." I danced all day and my energy rose and rose and rose. I found myself able to dance now with intent.

This began early in the morning. The trees all poked their heads over the top of the arbour and called to me. I began to blow the whistle in praise of the nature worlds. I began to dance to create the meditation vision I had a few months ago where the Tree was a fountain from which issued the four colours of the medicine wheel in the form of branches. Below the ground, the brown roots made a reverse fountain that dived down and then returned to the surface. The branches descended and the roots rose and they met at ground level to form some sort of dynamo. To achieve the vision of the coloured fountain I danced the colour of each direction and visualized an environment from that direction that typified the colour. I began with the West and danced Black; I danced the plains of America black with buffalo. In the South, I danced White and visualized the Antarctic. In the East, I danced Yellow and visualized the Sahara desert. I hoped my geography was correct. In the North, I danced Red and danced for the lava fields and volcanoes of Iceland. The local trees crowded in and the colour Green spread everywhere. A swan flew over, and all day the birds that flew over, pigeons, crows, seagulls, starlings, and swallows, lifted me and generated in me the energy of joy.

As I danced the fountains above and felt the trees draw near, I saw that the palms of my hands were glowing with the colour green. Circles of green filled the centres of my palms; they were not spheres lying on my hands but circles of energy in the palms of my hands and this was healing energy. I danced my palms and drew energy from the Tree into them and sent it out again to the world. I began to dance the root system of my vision, but I could not make it happen. I was puzzled: maybe it was because this Tree had no roots. I thought at one point it was beginning, then suddenly the Chief called an end to the dance round.

After the following rest period, as each round started I would hear a word and I would dance in honour of that word. The first word was 'Tolerance'. In the next dance, the word was 'Peace'. As I was dancing Peace, I saw in my inner vision a vertical crack appear in the Tree. This crack opened up. I was wearing my blanket poncho because the day had started off chilly. Suddenly I was very hot. I went to my place and threw it off, returning to dance on the spot where I had been before and looking intently at this crack.

Would I go now? .... or would I wait? ..... maybe even until tomorrow? ...... pushing the limits. Suddenly the Moon Mother was stood right behind me saying: "Are you going to go?" I said: "I am." I threw myself at the Tree. I fell backwards, my knees on either side of the trunk. I could feel the smooth beauty of the Tree, all was exactly as it should be; the Tree grew out of my lower centres, a great column of ascending light.

The helpers came and picked me up in a white sheet and carried me back to my place and that was a perfect moment. They left me and I experienced Peace. That was the gift that was given to me then. I understood what Peace felt like and why it would be so wonderful if all people could find Peace. In the next dance, I danced 'Happiness'.

I woke up during the night. Three energy points, the centre of seeing, the heart, and the generative centre, were all being energised at the same time. I felt sure that this was the first time this had happened in more than one centre at once. It was the most wonderful tingling feeling of incoming energy and the experience filled me with ecstasy. I felt so blessed that I could hardly accept I deserved it.

I felt very tired when we got up on Monday morning, but I still had the energy to dance. We had danced two or three rounds when suddenly I noticed that my vision of the fountains above and below was now present and complete. It had happened at some point that I was not aware of. As I danced, I heard this: "Till the end of Time." I understood that this kind of spiritual dance and interchange between incarnate and discarnate Beings would continue until the end of time and also that I would be there, dancing.

The time for the Dance came to an end and the Chief brought us each a drink of water, telling us to sit with it for half an hour before we drank it. In fact, I did not feel desperately thirsty, and I realized that I was not desperately hungry either.

When the Dance was over, we went to the medicine tipi where the Chief told us not to share our process for at least six months. He asked us if we had ever experienced the loss of the power of a dream when we told it to someone else. As this had been my frequent experience when I was younger and used to tell my dreams more carelessly, I took his advice very seriously. Afterwards the Dance Tree was felled, with the chain saw, and then we were called to the feast. Before I left the site, my car loaded with stuff to go back into Manchester, I went to the oak tree again and sat there for a while. A treecreeper came and cleaned the branch just above my head; hanging upside-down, it worked its way methodically along the entire length.

I got horribly lost on my way to the Manchester address. I noticed that the car's battery light had come on and would not go off. The car was likely to stop dead at any moment as I took several wrong turnings trying to find the right exit off the motorway. Eventually I got to the house where it transpired that the fan belt was missing. This made me decide to stay the night: my battery was obviously running flat.

On the way back from Manchester the day after the Dance, I went to visit the Apple tree. When I meditated just now, I found that as I had sat there I had entered into the tree. I experienced this again in the meditation. I experienced the marvellous rotational growth of the branches, which appeared to me to be like a vortex drawing down energy from above. I experienced the beautiful pink flowers that appear in the canopy in the spring and saw what they look like, viewed from above, in the green canopy of the wood, saw how they attract and feed the insects, and understood what a beautiful nurturing Being the Apple tree is. Carried by the vortex I reached ground level and passed into the root system. As I descended, the nature worlds became available to me most strongly. I saw and felt the greatness of the underground of the planet. Then I returned to ground level and saw that the point where trunk enters the ground is the exact place of the centre of generation. In contrast to the roots and branches, the generative centre, which marks the join between above and below, radiates outwards at ground level in a flat disc. From the centre of that horizontal disc, I saw a jet black spiral descending and expanding as it moved downwards. From the same point, I saw a bright yellow spiral ascending and expanding as it moved upwards. Their starting points were at ground level. When fully visible to me, they transformed and became the two wings of a butterfly, which landed on the Oak tree at the sacred site of the Sun Moon Dance.

the oak tree at the dance site

One evening, after work, about two weeks later, I went for a walk locally and I was so glad to get out. Not walking on the earth was making me ill and as I walked down the tarmac road, my feet were really hurting. The minute I crossed the stile onto the earth path all the pain went away. I went up to the hollow Ash tree. As I approached the tree, a very tiny rabbit was knocking around on its own outside the warren. Finding its re-entry to the burrow blocked by me, it freaked out, thumping the ground and making several false runs, all useless gestures that made me laugh.

I looked into the hollow trunk and I saw that there was a little bundle of feathers in the base of the tree. I put my hand through the hole in the base and pulled out the body of a baby owl, it was so decayed that it looked like a lump of earth with wings. I wondered if it was this year's hatchling. If so, I was amazed how quickly it had amalgamated itself into the ground. I felt a bit sad and wondered whether, if I had gone there on the right day, I would have found it alive and cherished it.

I walked on towards the wood. From some distance I could hear noisy knocking, I entered quietly and had a very clear view of the woodpecker industriously cleaning one of the trees, and all the time I was in the wood I could hear it working on one tree or another, darting here and there, until the wood became quite stereophonic. The echoes created by the sounds of hollowing were mesmerising and I meditated among the birch trees for a while, disappearing there in praise of the green trees.

As I left the wood, I felt deeply in love with the forms of the trees in a very heart-oriented way. I walked across the field. The light from the sun was strong. I approached the bank and hedge on the far side. About twelve rabbits were playing there, enjoying this low evening sun. Of course, they went to ground when they saw me. I apologised to them saying: "It is only one night this year that I will ruin your evening." The sun was shining directly onto the bank and onto a tree, which was split at ground level into five equal trunks. One of the trunks curved down over the banking and then grew upwards. I sat with my legs on either side of it. It was directly between me and the brilliant sun, which was about to drop behind the wood. I began to feel the light energising my centres and, feeling it, I opened them up.

This became a miraculous experience because the sunlight penetrated my energy centres and so did the energy of the tree: input from above and below. As my throat centre opened, a little breeze came into the branches of the tree and rattled the leaves. The sound energized my body and enlivened my mind. It was a moment of indescribable beauty. The sun became so brilliant that the light was the colour of white gold. My body relaxed completely and I felt wonderful.

As I stood up from this experience, my overwhelming feeling was that I had allowed myself to forget that the world was a place where you could experience ecstasy. That is what I said to the Sun; I said: "I forgot, I forgot!" I forgot that what I just felt was available, yes. I couldn't believe I had allowed myself to eradicate ecstasy from my life. It was as if I had done it in a fit of peak, refusing to allow myself to feel again because I had been hurt.

When I came back from the fields, the cars on the road were so loud as they roared past me that I thought: "Is this way of life really a substitute for the feeling that I have just experienced?" I came in and ate and then I went to bed. It was only half past nine, but I was so energised and so wiped out by the experience that I did not want to do anything else. I lay in bed and the owl, which visits the village, came very close and shouted: "-ifty, -ifty, -ifty." Then a car roared through with loud music playing and drowned out the sound of the owl, and this happened again and again. A huge lorry came through and I felt that the sound of these engines overcame the quieter subtleness of the other world. Was the thrill of the moving vehicle and the noise it made in any way spiritual for the people who experienced it? Because, you know, all life is said to be spiritual, so was that? I couldn't see that it was, and I wished that it did not drown out the voice of the owl, but I didn't feel anger towards the people, I just wondered if the trade-off was worth it.

At the weekend, I went out onto the Fell and I took my wooden flute because I wanted to play at a particular place below a tall waterless fall on the upper reaches of the river. The particular place is a thirty-foot diameter bowl at the base of a dry waterfall, encircled by natural stone walls about thirty feet high. I call it the Stone Temple. The only entrance is a narrow opening in the rock face where the river might occasionally run after heavy rain. To play the flute there was my plan, but Fate had other ideas; today everyone who was out on the Fell was walking up the river bed. The place was like the M6. Before I even thought about playing, two men came into the temple. I had a chat to them and then they climbed up the dry waterfall and away.

I noticed that the water level in the bowl during the storm, which had happened earlier in the week, must have been at least three feet; there was river foam stuck to the rocks at that height. I also found a sheep's bone, which I had previously hidden in a crevice, way over at the other side of the pool circle. The flood must have washed it out and eventually it must have been deposited by the eddying water. That gave me some indication of the water turbulence.

Then I did play my flute and this drew a solitary man into

my net, a schoolteacher out walking to get rid of the stress of paperwork. He tried to climb the dry fall, changed his mind, retraced his steps and went another way. This shows the value of companions because both of the earlier walkers got up it.

I realize that I have not recorded anything about the storm last Monday that I just mentioned. It had rained all night and by morning, still raining hard, the river levels were critical. I went to a remote village to see a customer, driving in as the local river covered the road to my wheel arches, feeling the terrifying pull of the current on the body of the car. I was too nervous to drive out that way again and went home via another route. This again was a frightening drive. The stone walls on the road sides formed channels for the water which ran in rivers down the tarmac and collected in the dips of the road. It was impossible to tell how deep the water was in these dips. I managed to get through but I was really freaked out. Being washed into the river by the current was a very terrifying prospect, but there would be nothing nice about stalling and wading through icy water, either.

Before I got seriously frightened, I had thought how great it would be to go up the Fell. Surely, the stony river bed would be a torrent of water and the towering dry waterfalls would be spectacular cascades? But by the time I got home I felt sure I would not be able to get there in the car. Judging by the state of the road when I went up on Sunday, I was right. The verges were seriously washed out, becoming channels that were about two feet deep. It looked as if vast torrents of water had poured down the road, never mind down the river itself.

Year Four

On my way to the next seminar led by my Teacher at the Foundation, I stopped halfway to spend the night in the Loch Leven Hotel. The view from my window was of the place where the waters of the river Leven mingle with the waters of the sea loch. Once before, when I stayed here, I looked out of the window in the morning and saw that the water was running upstream, a sight that quite unnerved me till I realized that the tide was coming in.

Today we are halfway through the seminar, which is focused on spiritual healing, and this morning we were asked to say how we were by means of a number from 1-10. I decided that I was at number 8, poised on the point of becoming 9. It was a moment of balance, of movement with security. As I was feeling this, a great change took place. It was of an indescribable sort, but the focus of interest shifted up to my heart without leaving my lower centres and I felt aware in my spirit body at the level of my heart.

Resting in my room later, I lay in a very steady state of deep happiness. I looked forward in time to a place where I had moved north and left my old life in the west. Although the details of it were not clear, nor the pains that I might encounter on the way accounted for, in the meditative state it seemed exactly the right move and I should never allow any of the difficult aspects of it to destroy the intense and wonderful feeling that it gave me. I would describe the feeling as 'divine longing', so named in one of Joseph's books.

I thought for a while about the longing for the divine. I thought that the great trick of successful spiritual practice is to be able to stand it! Yes, stand the intensity of the longing without going off the rails completely, stand it and try to understand it. At the end of the meditation, I saw a seashore with white foam wavelets running in regular bands onto a sandy beach. From this image, I understood that sexuality is here-ness and that sexuality is the expression of divine longing in the physical world. That is why sexual feelings are deeply enmeshed with the spiritual, because they are divine longing expressing itself in our physical Beings. Yes, I sound like a Crone.

In the early evening, I tried to rest and meditate but it did not work out. I felt very peculiar, driven but exhausted. In the end, I decided I needed to take the hand drum, which I had brought with me, out into nature. I walked slowly through the dunes and, after a while, I sat, feet on the ground, on the low-growing branch of a birch tree. Some very, very strange sensations occurred in my lower centres and I felt extremely dizzy. This went on for a while as I surrendered my energy to the tree and as I received in exchange the tree energy, and our energies combined.

I took the drum and began to play. When I finished playing I put the drum face down on the ground, saying: "I dedicate this drum to the hollow tree." I put the drumstick down on the ground, saying: "I dedicate this drumstick to the bones of the Grandfather." Then I laid myself face down on the ground and I said: "I dedicate myself to Father-Mother-Earth-Life."

This entirely correct set of dedications marked the conclusion of my quest for sexual and emotional healing. It was done and I came to the Nature sanctuary in the fading light. I lit the candle and drummed there. It was as if I brought something from the outside, from the dedication ceremony, into the sanctuary, for, as I drummed, I saw great Tree Beings marching into view from some distantly hidden place. They were quite awesome but I carried on drumming; after them, a Child of Light was brought and became a fire in the centre of the circle that those Great Beings had made.

The Ascending Spiral

The next evening we took a journey, not to the beat of the drum this time but to music on a cd, a journey to our inner temple.

I found myself walking towards and entering into a very large tree, entering into the golden space that exists within the tree. In the centre of this tree-space there was a nodule on the ground, something like what I imagine the pituitary gland to look like; it looked like a little mushroom, or like a table-shaped internal growth of the wood of the tree growing up from the ground like a platform. I knelt and put my forehead on this platform in an attitude of praying. I was quite happy if I simply stayed there for the entire journey because the visual intensity of the brown tree and the goldenness within was so pleasing.

But when the music started, two Coyotes came and began to dance in a very stately way around the circular space where I knelt in the middle. I looked up and they became two spiralling columns, shining black and translucent yellow. Then, as they slowly rose in twisting, curling columns of light, I saw the colour pink appear and turn with them, then the colour blue and then green, so that there were five columns of translucent light turning like smoke and rising upwards. I found that I was rising with them. The most overwhelming sensation of joy came into me; my stomach began to tremble, my rib cage began to heave, and I wanted to cry out loudly under the intensity of this agonisingly beautiful experience of rising in the columns of light. I became so intensely emotional that I thought I couldn't go on. I had lost sight of the Coyotes. I cried out to them: "Where are you?" and they said: "We are making this Tree for you. Don't worry, we are still here, we are making this Tree."

The overpowering feeling diminished and I began to see a bowl made of blue and yellow petals with crystal-like quality. I was resting in the centre of this bowl. The bowl began to turn, very slowly, anticlockwise and move off to the left. As it moved, it closed over me and the colours changed from blue and yellow to black and yellow. I was held within this black and yellow ball. It moved out and up to the left and I was able to see the entire shape and structure of the Tree, the branches radiated out from the trunk in a great circling, clockwise sweep. A shape like the image of a galaxy was formed as the branches grew out and upwards to the sky.

The black and yellow ball took me outside the periphery of the Tree to circle in orbit. I was held within the ball, but I was conscious outside of it and from outside I watched. I saw the arms and legs and tails and snouts of different animals emerge from the ball. I saw the arms and feet of a kangaroo. Then I saw the hands and feet of a shrew-like creature, its nose and tail also peeped out. These images continued and I could have stayed and watched as every single four-limbed creature emerged in part from this sphere and then disappeared into it again.

I thought about the journey and I wondered: "What is the purpose of it?" I began again to feel agony, of a different sort to ascending the spirals of light, the agony of a painless but pointless existence. I felt this more and more, so I looked down again towards the Tree. In the space created above the crown, I could see big birds circling. I looked into the centre of the vortex there and I could see that the coloured columns of light travelling up the trunk of the Tree were coming out of the top in a great rising spiral, creating thermals for these enormous birds to soar upon. I came into the consciousness of one of these birds, a most gigantic Condor. It was circling without effort, higher and higher and higher, on the heat from the centre of the Tree. I looked down and I saw the other birds far below. I circled up, up, up on the thermal column, way, way, way beyond any images.

Then I saw a Great Hand that was closed into a fist. The fingers were the columns of gigantic stone cliffs. I flew towards the vertical faces of these cliffs. There was no ledge for a bird to land on. Gliding with the cliffs to my right I noticed that streamers of wispy cloud were floating on my left-hand side. I flew into these clouds. As I flew on, I became more and more wispy myself until I lost consciousness of the form of the bird and became cirrus-cloud. I wondered: "What is this for?" but without any joy, or agony, or any feeling now. I debated with myself what I could do, because I kept looking back and farther and farther away was the Tree and the World. I formed a plan. I thought that I could condense as rain and fall upon the earth, but my heart wasn't into doing that.

As I was thinking: "No, I don't want to descend, however altruistic that might be." I happened to glance up and I saw that the Condor was above, flying higher, still higher. I saw that the two Coyotes were in the Condor and I went up to join them. We went higher. When we reached a certain height an immense Spiritual Feeling entered my body; it had no form, no image, and no colour, nothing but a feeling. It came into me further and further and further and I just kept staying with it, holding onto it.

The music came to an end and in no way did I want to return but eventually the two Coyotes did tug at me and I turned my attention to them. They condensed themselves into a ball around me again and, in this way, we came back without too much agony.

On my return I thought that the dedication I made the day before to Mother-Father-Earth-Life applies to my meditative travels in this way: to make the effort to record them onto tape as soon as I return and later to type them up in case they may someday be helpful to people. I realized that there is a laziness in me that hopes to avoid the effort involved in recording the travels I take, and that overcoming inertia is really what dedication is all about: that is what the personal contribution is.

Four months passed and it was late May when, as I began to meditate, I found myself walking up the lower part of the river going to the Ash tree over the water. I lay on that tree against the shaggy green moss that covers the bark, my body opened up and I began to enter the tree. I remembered what that tree has given me, and the tree responded: "Be like me, stand firm and draw the power." I recalled that a tree draws power from above and from below.

I looked down into the water of the stream running past below the horizontal trunk and I entered the water, travelling against the flow, upstream, so that I reached the place where the small dry hollow sits beside the waterfall that fills the pool. I went there once and the entrance was covered with a spider's web. Now drops from the falling water had spangled the web, and the fact that it was intact meant that no creature had entered that little cave recently.

I went in there now and, in the darkness of that place, my friend and business associate, who is seriously ill with bone marrow cancer, began to arrive very strongly in those colours that belong with him, black and purple and brown. All I had to do was concentrate on the feeling and the image of him, as it circulated in the cave, and a healing would take place. There were three phases to this process: he came very strongly and filled the cave, then his image faded; it returned and retreated again, and then it returned for a third time. I prayed that by holding that space I had helped my friend.

Beautiful Painted Arrow, Joseph Rael, encourages people to create ceremony, teaching that ceremony is a way to express willingness, commitment, and gratitude. Ceremony brings the known and the unknown together in a way that makes communication between them more possible. For example, during a sweat lodge, Joseph received a request from the Spirit of the Waters asking that a Fire Ceremony be held for the purification of the Oceans on the seventh of each month. The Ocean Spirit asked him to teach the ceremony to other people so that it could be done in many places, as the need was great.

The first time I participated in the Fire Ceremony it was done in this way: a square stack of twenty-eight sticks was built and blessed with tobacco and maize, representing the Ancestors, Grandfathers and Grandmothers, who would be there to bless our endeavour. The fire was then lit and we watched it burn until the sticks were ash. The wood of the fire burning brightly for the purification of all the oceans: the cosmic ocean, the oceans of water, and the oceans of thought in our individual minds; the heat transforming wood into flame, matter into movement, the static into rising light. While the wood burned, we were encouraged to look into the fire for insights, and I found peace.

Last night was the night for the Fire Ceremony. The day had been hectic, and had ended with me going into town to look for a washing machine as ours had broken down and the insurance was insisting we had a new one. When I came back I didn't feel I could achieve everything I needed to do. But I did achieve, and, a little later than planned, I got ready to go out to do the ceremony.

A couple of years ago my partner and I had made some alterations to our house, removing the wall between the kitchen and dining room and making new kitchen cupboards out of californian pitch pine which we bought from a local recycling business. The baulks of timber were from a demolished victorian mill and we were told that wood from this particular species was logged out during that era. It proved to be a beautiful wood, the grain full of sunny orange and yellow colours, a lovely scent of fresh pine, and very easy to work. For the fire-stack, I collected up the off-cuts from the last kitchen cupboard, just completed.

I headed over the fields to the Ash tree where I saw the three power animals, wanting to perform the ceremony there. As I walked, I realized that in my hurry I had forgotten to bring any paper; I had matches and a bundle of dried leaves, but would these really ignite the sticks? For days, the weather had been rain on rain and everything was sodden.

the hollow in the tree

I laid my head against the trunk and shut my eyes, stretching my consciousness into the body of that hollow tree. The whole shape of space changed. The ground began to slip and the world was tipping. When everything settled down I sat on the ground with my back to the trunk just waiting for the right time, sometimes I had my eyes closed and sometimes I had them open, there was no rush at all. The shadow of a bird flew to the tree. It was the tawny owl. As it landed, the hissing cry of owlets was clearly audible. I sat very still and I don't think the owl saw me, but nor did I see where it landed. I thought it must have left immediately and, after a minute or two, I stood up ready to begin the fire ceremony; startled, it flew out of the tree to a fence post close by. It sat there unafraid, bobbing and staring at me.

The imminent ceremony, the presence and power of the owl, and the hollow column within the tree, flooded my mind. I was very excited at the prospect of lighting the fire there, at the base of the lightning-struck tree, but then I thought: "The owl is not very far away. Lighting a fire so close to her nest is not a good thing to do. What if she becomes so horrified that she abandons the nest, or the owlets have to leave and become vulnerable, and what about the effect of the smoke?" Never having burnt any of the wood before, I had no idea what sort of fire it was going to be. I decided that I would not hold the ceremony there.

I went into the wood. As I entered, I saw that the bluebell flowering was over and the ground was a gelatinous mass of rotting bluebell leaves. It was so slippery underfoot that as I tried to walk up a slight incline my feet kept slipping and sliding back down, I was literally stuck in one place. Hanging onto the trees and bushes, I managed to get up the slope to where the ground was flatter.

As I searched for the correct place, it was awesome in the wood and my senses were wide awake. I noticed a little tunnel at the base of a likely tree stump and I remembered that I had once seen busy shrews darting about there. I worried: "Here too I may disturb a creature with my fire." It seemed to me that the wood was full of living creatures and that, really, there was no place for me in their world. But eventually, I found a spot and laid the fire.

The stack was a chaotic mess, like a badly built tower block. I thought: "It cannot possibly stand for long." I used about ten matches trying to light it, but eventually the dry leaves lit and the flames quickly caught hold of the sticks. There was not a breath of wind and the flames of the californian pitch pine burned in a very concentrated bright yellow block. It was a very sobering thought that this species of tree might be extinct. As I leave my kitchen behind will the new owners just pull it out and let it go to the tip, this precious wood that could serve us for so long?

The flames seemed to float in the air above the burning wood, unattached to the smouldering sticks. As their intensity decreased, they burned more orange but still very single coloured. When they eventually died down, the glowing embers began to give off a column of smoke that came in puffs as if someone was breathing there in the fire. This was a strange phenomenon. I couldn't understand why the smoke didn't come in a continuous stream. The air in the wood was very clear, and crystal clarity was apparent outside of the column of smoke that pulsed consistently in one direction. Eventually, the time came; I made sure the ash was cool and came home.

When I had built the pile of sticks, I laid a maize circle and a tobacco circle round them, praying first to the Grandmothers and then to the Grandfathers to help me, because I am so ignorant. As I looked at the wobbling pile of sticks, which, by the way, never did fall over but collapsed vertically without losing the square shape, I just thought how incompetent I was, struggling to find the spirit world in this speedy and ignore-ant time.

Year Five

I left the west and moved north. Today when the Grandfather was with me, everything was spiritual and contained the colour Blue and all became one in the Blue. I saw the Sun Moon Dance Tree; the Tree was the Great Mother and within her hollow body, all things could be made.

With the Sun Moon Dance Tree in front of me and with the colour yellow very present, I came to meditate. As I approached, the Y-shaped Tree was black against the yellow background. The Tree fell into pieces, and collapsed in a circle on the ground of the arbour. As it fell, I heard: "Eight pieces." And certainly there were eight black logs there. With my effort I began to re-build the Tree; four of the logs formed the trunk, and two formed each arm. The remade Tree stood upright again in the centre. On the ground below lay my body, also a Y-shape but different to the Tree. The Tree's branches stretched upwards, while my legs, which made the Y-shape in my body, stretched downwards, and, when I was standing, they touched the earth, but, at this moment, I was horizontal. The Tree was growing out of my navel centre and the place where the vertical touched the horizontal was blue.

The Tree is Never Separated

Sunday I went into the pine forest to collect sticks and I came across a strange sight. A tall thin tree had broken and, falling from a higher piece of ground, its branches had become enmeshed in other trees growing lower down the slope so that its trunk now hung in space and, moved by the wind, swung like a pendulum. On a shamanic level, it horrified me because it was so strange to see a tree, in our world of everyday, hanging and moving in that way.

Eventually I exchanged my fear for bravado, and stood beneath this suspended tree whose diameter was about five or six inches. By inches, I was exactly the right height to stand under it without the trunk touching me. I stayed there, feeling the random movement of the tree circulating over my head. There was the possibility that at any moment it could drop.

A Black Bear, a great authority on trees, and I were heading towards a distant forest and as we walked we discussed the nature of trees. I began: "Why is it that trees do not seem to suffer pain?" "Yes, they do not suffer the pains of the ego. They do not suffer the pains caused by interaction between themselves and others." "Why is that?" "Because they are not separated from the earth like all the Beings with legs, who suffer with an individual kind of pain that trees do not have." "Oh, so it is because the tree is never separated from its Mother the Earth."

The image of an acorn came. The Bear ate the acorn, and my questioning mind asked: "What about the acorn? That is not always attached to Mother Earth." It was the listening spirits who replied: "No, you are wrong, because at first it is attached to the tree and it is a part of the tree, then there is only a very brief moment when it leaves the tree and descends and lands upon the earth. That is the only moment that it is not connected to the Earth Mother, and in that time it is falling towards her, and if, for a brief moment, there is a separation there, it really isn't separation because the acorn has only one way to go in its intent, which is down and into the Mother's body." I was satisfied with this. The trees are never separated from their Mother the Earth.

I saw a Great Tree fall in the forest. The minute it lay horizontally upon the forest floor, instead of only being connected to the Mother by its root centre, all of its centres reconnected into the earth there and it began to become soil and to be the nourishing home of many Beings.

I found myself then in the Sun Moon Dance arbour approaching union with the Tree. "Look, Spirits, this Tree has been cut from its roots and it does not lie horizontally on the earth. What is the spiritual nature of this Tree?" As I touched the Tree, they showed me the special nature of the Dance Tree. How this Tree is artificially separated from the Mother and placed vertically in the ground without roots. How there is a special function for this Tree which is to help the rootless person to reach into the light.

This morning I found myself standing next to a large stone ball, one of a pair of the sort that top the gateways of very grand houses. I didn't particularly like seeing it there in the landscape of the travelling body and I thought: "I need a power animal to help me roll this away." A stone Lion appeared, a very strange idea of a power animal to me, but it soon became clear that this was the proud Lion, who had once placed his foot upon the stone ball. Together we pushed the heavy ball and it rolled away down a slight incline and dropped into the void. Hum, did I mind that it was disappearing for ever? No, I had not been very fond of it anyway. Underneath where it had been, I noticed a very small golden hole that had previously been obscured by the stopper of stone. The stone Lion and I looked at each other. I scrutinized his archetypal victorian form, redolent of empire, always a male Lion, and I said to him: "I think you and I had better go through that hole."

I went first and then encouraged him to follow. As he squeezed through he was transformed into a living Lion because the world that we entered was the world of golden light, and, not only did he become a lithe, golden Lion, but he became a Lioness. In the golden world, we were able to be one and, as one, we stepped forward. Hah, I was full of expectations about what glorious realms of light we might visit, but, to my surprise, I saw that we were approaching civilisation and I wondered: "How will this Lioness get on in a city?"

Suddenly we were in a gloomy smithy. The air was thick and hot; a bright fire raged in the furnace, a pair of bellows stood to hand. Examining the metalwork that was stacked up there, I realized: "Wow, we came from the Stone Age and we have entered the Iron Age." Glancing around, I saw that the lion-ess-ence was no longer there; I was standing in the blacksmith's shop on my own. I hesitated for a moment: "Should I go on alone?" Then I stepped through the wall of the shop into another dimension.

I was approaching a forest, admiring the tall-standing trees, when the image of a chainsaw came, so noisy, so lethal, and so rapid. My thoughts too were rapid: "As time goes on, faster and faster ways of felling trees are appearing; and faster and faster the forests are disappearing, all in the name of the march of progress." I did not want to cut down the mighty trees, there was plenty of wood lying on the ground all around that had fallen from them and I was thinking: "Why don't I just use this wood?"

At that moment, I saw a plastics factory belting out its waste products into the atmosphere, and I realized that I had stepped from the Iron Age into the Industrial Age. People say planting more trees will ease the effects of the factories and their products on the environment, especially the effects on the atmosphere, but, in so many ways, factories consume trees. In fact, when I think about it, all that we do is consume trees. When bidden, did I not eat the tree? I wondered: "What is this march of progress?"

The scene changed and I found myself in a strangely beautiful, simple world. An ancient Oak tree occupied the left-hand side of the circular view that I had of this world. The bole of the Oak was knotty and distorted but immensely wide and strong. In the rest of the circle a moon-coloured light was evident and not much else. The delicate light occupied a little more than half of this world and the knotty wood of the tree filled the rest.

I fixed my attention on the place where the tree met the light and I laid my awareness there, slowly I was drawn into the heart of the tree. The tree centre was full of coloured lights rising upwards. How gnarled, convoluted and darkly brown was the outside of the tree and yet, how fluid and spectacularly gorgeous were the lights within, and how straight their lines of ascent.

I entered into the stream, travelling up the lines of liquid light. I encountered the round shape of a creature there and I entered joyfully into the body of the Owl. I was rising without effort, but part of my consciousness still stood at the base of the tree. I looked up to see three or four Owls sitting at the top of the tree and I knew that I must never take my eyes off those Owls because when I looked again they would have flown and there would not have been a single sound to alert me when they left.

My journey moved on, and I saw a number 9 in the next frame of the film that was playing before me. The number 9 was a spiral going anticlockwise: the movement coming up from its tail and turning round the roundness of the top to end in the centre. I was trying to understand why I should suddenly see a 9 when I came back to my daily consciousness, realizing that I had taken a trip through the history of humanity and that, along the way, I had discovered, in the eternal need for wood, that the trip was a kind of standing still. All those named 'Ages' were one long Wood Age sustained by Trees. Then I remembered that if you add together the individual numbers in multiples of 9 they always add up to 9. And now I notice that when the multiples of 1 to 10 x 9 are placed in a line, they form a palindrome:

09 18 27 36 45 54 63 72 81 90

Year Six

From the Vast Form of the Earth

What follows may be a rather rambling story, but you must be used to that. It was a most ethereal experience and one that I would normally not put on the tape because I would not be able to make it coherent, but this morning I have decided to try.

In my meditation, I was calling quietly to the Ancestors. I called: "Grandfathers!" paused, and called: "Grandmothers!" A field opened up in front of me in another dimension and I saw many Ancestors standing in that field. Standing in grass, which was about up to their waists, they were all quietly looking downwards. "What are they doing?" I decided to join them and, rather than interrupting them with any questions, I adopted the same position of standing quietly in the field of grass.

I saw that the colours of the place were green and blue and yellow. These colours, blue, green, and yellow, are the central colours of the rainbow: "This must be a teaching from the rainbow." Looking at the rainbow, I saw that the red and the orange, on one side, and the indigo and the violet, on the other, protect and enclose the three colours in the centre, and that those three colours are where we exist. From then on the meditation led me. Consequently, I am only left with little pockets of awareness.

I met some extraordinary huge Trees, of which there were four. I felt that they were the Spirits of the Directions. They didn't have trunks like normal trees; their bodies were extremely broad and knobbly, the branches were much smaller and not the main focus of the energy. It must have been through the mediumship of these Trees that I reached the edge of our perception, the edge of our world, the edge of our universe.

There I found a Tree, its roots in our world. I climbed this Tree and out onto the particular branch which grew beyond the limits of our perception and, needless to say, whatever I saw there has completely disappeared, but I do remember going out upon that limb. In the end I was talking to some very wise Beings. They said something to me so sensible, so obvious, I felt I could never forget it, but, again, I have. I think it was something like: "This is what we have been doing all along." They were talking about what I had just been doing in the meditation: trying to expand the limits of my awareness.

Lying here, I noticed that my heartaches were absent. I felt absolutely brilliant, my awareness was wide open and extensive, and I thought how the journey could not be talked about in a linear, logical, sensible manner. I thought how ironic it was that I entered the place of non-sense and felt better, felt wonderful there, whereas in the sensible world I am, at the moment, feeling uncomfortable, not able to relax, and, often, in pain.

Those Spirits in the Field were contemplating the earth. They were looking down towards the ground, and what they were doing was contemplating and being absorbed in the earth, our Earth, in some great mission of expanding awareness, which is what our Mother, the Vast Self, is doing here.

I had the feeling that we are holding the vast form of the Earth in our hands. How can this be, when each of us is such a small speck upon the surface? But I could accept, and it was important for me to accept, that there is a place of Greatness where we do hold the Vast Self in our hands.

welcoming the sunrise

Abouts

About Teachers

I am writing about Teachers and yet before I met my Teacher I had given up on the concept. Then in meeting one, I found two: my Teacher, Alexander, and his Teacher, Joseph.

My Teacher, from a european background, enabled me to connect to parts of myself which I had not explored before, which I had not even known existed, and that widening view of what I am is helping me to re-examine my life, my expression of myself and my contribution to consciousness. In the process, my malfunctioning parts are getting fixed.

His Teacher, from a native american background, has a more public face. He has made a body of Teachings that are available to everyone through books, videos, cds and artwork. From visions he received, he has given ceremonies and initiated the building of sound peace chambers to help us reach our full potential, as all life strives to do.

These Teachers give me everything I need to remain in love with life and to be inspired to make the effort to contribute what I can to tolerance, peace and happiness. They do not tell me what I should do, or how I must behave; they give me some guidelines and ask me to take responsibility for my thoughts and my actions.

Joseph is the bowl,
Alexander is the water in the bowl,
I am the thirsty person who could hold the bowl and take a drink.

I say a grateful thank you to my Teachers in human form.

About a Paradox

If it comes to a choice between predestination and free will, I would choose free will. Even if it does not exist, I would still opt for it because without it I can't see the point of being alive. However, since I have gained access to what, for want of better words, might be called 'altered states of consciousness' I have had some experiences which hint that the paradox is not what it seems.

When I write a book, I search through my meditation records, abstract the parts that resonate with the subject and work with them to make the story, staying as true as I can to the original text. Sometimes, when I go through the material, I get quite a surprise.

One of those surprises is in this book, in the content of the meditative experience at the beginning of Year Five where the Dance Tree falls into eight pieces and is re-assembled by me. At the time that I experienced it, I was a Sun Moon dancer and it seemed to be a dedication of myself to the Tree. It was mysterious though, for example, why did the Tree fall into eight pieces?

Two years later, and not expecting it, I became chief and I held the Dance for several years. Then I handed the chief-ness on. It was another few years before I collected together the material to write this book. At the same time, I wrote up the history of the Sun Moon dance in the UK, discovering that I had chiefed eight dances, and so, both things being in my mind at the same time, the number eight fell into place!

Now, was that, as a foreseeing, an example of predestination or, as a personal commitment, an example of free will? It could not be a foreseeing because I didn't see it, and it could not be free will because I didn't desire it. It was neither. It was an example of the vastness of awareness manifesting within the limitations of time.

About Time and the Timeless

Always embedded in my books there is the thin thread of a timeline. It is there to give a sense of time passing, because that is how things happen in the everyday world, where Time is the limiter.

When I laid my body down and withdrew my attention from that world, another body would become active where space seemed endless and time disappeared. Then experience became a very different thing. I no longer went out to collect experiences and they no longer impinged upon me. The sense of separation was gone, and goodness knows how or where the experiences happened but they did. I would call that place of consciousness, the Timeless.

Visiting the Timeless had a profound effect on my daily life; however stressed and under pressure I had been on entering the altered state when I returned I could better bear my life. So important, but for me the attraction was the mystery outside of Time.

If asked, I couldn't say what is real and what is not but I do know that the physical world is the foundation of all my experience. No matter how far my awareness can expand, I still need the physical, the world of breath, matter and movement, the world of forms. That world is the other enticing mystery, a mystery which I completely lost sight of, until I left it for a while.

There is a place where it is possible to be aware in both mysteries simultaneously, Joseph names it 'the Timeless Moment'. It is the instant of experiencing: it is the present.

As soon as I reflect on the present, my connection to the timeless is hidden. 'Thinking about' does not happen in the Timeless Moment, where there is no past and no future, no memory and no planning, and that is why no-one can say exactly where inspiration comes from or how it arrives.

Other Books by the Author

Tales of Two Coyotes: adventures with power animals

A great deal of fun and some profound suffering are the order of the day (and the night) in this book of 33 shamanic journeys taken while working with various groups of people in seminars led by my Teacher.

There are ten chapters in the book, each one introduced with a colour sketch.

Being of Earth

Loving the Buffalo from before I can remember, I am happy to travel through all times and all spaces in their company. I follow their wanderings until we come to the present moment: a place where the future is Green.

Colour sketches are included in the text as an aid to visualization.

contact the author: stella@peacechamber.co.uk
related websites: www.peacechamber.co.uk
  www.somethingdoeshappen.co.uk

list of contents and photographic images: *page*

        the face of the apple tree — *front cover*
        ash keys — *title page*
        a path through the forest — *iv*

Year One — 1
   Out of the Blue — 1
Year Two — 4
      the spiral mound — *8*
      birch trees in a spring sky — *11*
      the apple tree in winter — *12*
      the ash tree of the animals — *15*
      the ash tree over the water — *16*
      two fallen trees — *19*
      the ash tree from rock — *31*
   The Protection of Trees — 33
      treecreeper — *33*
      the spreading oak tree — *35*
      green velvet — *37*
      tawny owl — *39*
Year Three — 52
      inside the hollow tree — *55*
      great spotted woodpecker — *57*
      in the bluebell wood — *67*
   My Dance is a Tree — 70
      the dance tree — *73*
      the oak tree at the dance site — *83*
Year Four — 88
   The Ascending Spiral — 90
      the hollow in the tree — *95*
Year Five — 98
   The Tree is Never Separated — 98
Year Six — 103
   From the Vast Form of the Earth — 103
      welcoming the sunrise — *105*

www.ingramcontent.com/pod-product-compliance
Lightning Source LLC
Chambersburg PA
CBHW061802070526
44586CB00023B/2670